SARAH NELSON

A Perfect Storm

Devotions During A Crisis

Featured Guest Shelley Reeves

Second edition

ISBN: 978-0-578-85993-4

Cover art by Susan Graves

This book was professionally typeset on Reedsy.
Find out more at reedsy.com

Contents

Preface

Our crisis began in Park City, Utah on February 26, 2014. During a family ski trip, our two-year-old daughter, Adalee, suffered an ischemic stroke on the left side of her brain. Adalee lost her ability to speak, and the right side of her body was paralyzed. Adalee spent almost two weeks in a children's hospital in Salt Lake City and was transferred to a children's rehabilitation hospital in Dallas. We quickly learned every stroke is different, and there were no guarantees. Our family consists of myself, my husband Mark, our son Seth, our daughter Hannah Grace, and our daughter Adalee. During this time, our children were 7, 5, and 2.

I share this story as a testament of how the Lord revealed Himself to me and my family. As I was walking through this crisis, the Lord opened my eyes to help me see the many lessons He taught me along the way.

This devotional is based on scripture first, and then uses our story as a backdrop to demonstrate how God used His word and Holy Spirit to minister to us.

Journey to Write

Writing our story was a journey that took years to accept, process, and was completed in several stages. I welcome the opportunity to share how God revealed Himself and sustained us during a life-threatening crisis. At the same time, sharing our personal story is one of the most vulnerable things I have ever done. I dealt with fear, self-criticism, doubt, and procrastination permeated every fiber of my being. In the beginning, the difficult part was feeling compelled to share and write, while not having a clear understanding of how to move forward once this story was penned. I began to feel led to write this testimony during a time I was walking the rocky road of living it. I was navigating a crisis while trying to seek a purpose of why the Lord would impress on me to write it down. It was as if I was cautiously making my way through a thick fog. The journey of writing this story unfolded in real time as we were progressing through the actual circumstances.

It was during the time I was staying with Adalee in the hospital that I began to believe I was supposed to share her story. I felt impressed to share with others how the Lord revealed Himself to me. One of the reasons I felt led to share is because everyone faces hardship. I believe the Lord placed a sense of responsibility on my heart to share how He comforted us through a traumatic situation in order to encourage others. I did not initially have a sense of clarity, but as the story unfolds the Lord revealed to me how I would follow through on what He was telling me to do. I was processing a crisis with my two-year old baby girl and operating as a mother and care giver, while wading through a spiritual force I felt compelled to follow and understand. As I began to journal our crisis, I asked the Lord for confirmation. I continued to have many doubts about writing and had questions as to what format I should use. I am not an expert or a theologian. I am not an author, or a pastor, and I have had serious feelings of inadequacy. However, the Lord kept speaking to me through scripture to *simply... share.* One of the first scriptures the Lord led me to was Psalm 34. Our daughter experienced a life threatening and debilitating stroke, but the Lord gave her healing, restoration, and displayed His power to demonstrate what can happen when we have faith and call on others to pray on our behalf. To say I am forever grateful for her healing is an understatement, and I began to grasp that I was supposed to do what Psalm 34 avows.

Psalm 34: 1- 7

"I will extol the Lord at all times; His praise will always be on my lips; my soul will boast in the Lord; let the afflicted hear and rejoice. Glorify the Lord with me; let us exalt His name together.I sought the Lord, and He answered me; He delivered me from all my fears. Those who look to Him are radiant; their faces are never covered with shame. The poor man called, and the Lord heard him; He saved him out of all his troubles.The angel of the Lord encamps around those who fear Him, and he delivers them."

Psalm 34: 17 – 19

"The righteous cry out, and the Lord hears them; He delivers them from all their troubles.The Lord is close to the broken hearted and saves those who are crushed in spirit."

New International Version

I continued to crave tangible validation. I prayed diligently and the Lord graciously gave me affirmations through bible study, scripture, and continued to press in on me. I felt in the depths of my spirit God wanted me to write, but I was not sure how to begin. I had some major hold ups, and even though I believed the Holy Spirit was leading me I needed encouragement. I was chewing on the idea, thinking about it all the time, but had many reasons not to follow through. First, I did not know if I possessed the necessary skills and felt unqualified. I have faith God can do anything regardless of my shortcomings, but other reasons such as fear stifled me. I feared what people might think, and that it would appear I was trying to capitalize on a life-threatening event my child had to endure. As the fear continue to grip me, I prayed God would use someone in my life to offer me verbal assurance. I also began to feel it was time to seek advice, and to receive input from my husband.

On Valentine's Day 2015, almost one year from Adalee's stroke, Mark and I went on a date night to celebrate the romantic holiday. Over Italian cuisine in a tiny, crowded restaurant I shared how I believed God was leading me to tell our story. I trusted Mark's counsel and knew he would offer insight to help me ascertain whether this idea was from God, or a motherly response to processing a traumatic event. After listening to me intently, Mark looked at me and confidently said, *"You should write it as a devotional! That's the answer!"*. He was concise, deliberate, and saw it with clarity. I was taken back because the one detail I had not mentioned in the entire conversation was how the Lord laid it on my heart to write our story in the format of a devotional.

Once again, I received confirmation, but fear continued to intensify. I am not an "author", a natural born "story-teller", and did not feel equipped. However, the phrase that kept coming to mind was *"My weakness is God's Strength"*, and I knew I had to believe He would help me.

Another confirmation I received was found in scripture. Our new pastor at our church used the scripture 2 Corinthians 1: 3-5 in one of his sermons, and it solidified to me what I was feeling was biblical and from the Lord.

2 Corinthians 1: 3-5

"Praise be the God and Father of our Lord Jesus Christ, the Father of compassion and the God of all comfort, who comforts us in all our troubles, so that we can comfort those in any trouble with the comfort we ourselves have received from God."

New International Version

I have personally experienced the truth in this scripture. When we receive the Lord's comfort it allows us the privilege to share what God has done in our life, and in turn gives others the same comfort we ourselves have received. There have been several occasions where I have been able to speak and share how the Lord walked me through a crisis. Afterwards, countless people expressed how they can relate because of similar circumstances in their own lives. I share our family's story not because I think we are "special", or that our experience is beyond what others can comprehend. I do not share because I think I can bestow infinite "wisdom". If anything, there are so many more people who suffer and endure beyond what I can fathom. Because of our experience, I have taken a glimpse and seen suffering and difficulty in the faces of small, innocent children and their parents, and I know I have not even seen the half of it. I share our story because even as Christians we are not immune to hardships.

People relate to stories because our lives are made of them. Our chapters may look different in the details, but we all share in love, laughter, pain, and death. Real life stories inspire, encourage, and give us strength. Over the last few years, we have seen God's remarkable plan unfold and have witnessed how others were impacted by using our story to relate to family, friends, and strangers. I have continually been reminded of Psalm 34 and to give God the glory, not just for Adalee's recovery, but for how He revealed Himself to us and held us up during a difficult time. I pray that by simply sharing it will build the faith of others.

My prayer today is that you would be encouraged. If you are dealing with a crisis, I pray you would receive the Lord's peace in your life.

Salvation

Devotion 1

Romans 3:23-24

"**f**or all have sinned and fall short of the glory of God, and are justified by his grace as a gift, through the redemption that is in Christ Jesus."

English Standard Version

Life's circumstances are different for us all, but God's promise stays the same. The bible does not promise bad things will not happen, but it does promise God will always be with us. If you are dealing with difficulty or find yourself in a crisis there is a God who loves you. Peace is found when we accept Jesus Christ as our Savior. The first step is to believe that Jesus in the son of the living God, that He died for the atonement of our sins, was crucified, died, and was resurrected to new life. If we believe in Jesus, we can receive His grace through the sacrifice of His blood as a cleansing of our sins, and we can inherit eternal life with Christ in heaven.

1 Corinthians 5:3-4 "*...Christ died for our sins according to the Scriptures, that he was buried, that he was raised on the third day according to the Scriptures.*"

New International Version

Application

The bible says to confess your faith. Romans 10:9-10 says,"*That if you confess with your mouth, 'Jesus is Lord', and believe in your heart that God raised Him from the dead you are saved. For it is with your heart that you are believed and are justified, and it is with your mouth that you confess and are saved.*"

New International Version

The word "*justified*" means guiltless. Jesus gave his life on a cross to pay for our sins. He died in our place so that our sins can be forgiven. There is no one else who has shown such love as to lay down his own life for the world. John 3: 16 "*For God so loved the world he gave his one and only son, that whoever believes in him will not perish but have eternal life.*" If you already have a relationship with Jesus, be encouraged. He wants to continue to walk through this time with you. He is here to draw close to you, and to use your situation for good.

Romans 8:28 "*And we know that in all things God Works for the good of those who love him, who have been called according to his purpose.*"

New International Version

God also gives us eternal victory through our salvation. Jesus gives us hope, strength, and promises that nothing can separate us from His love.

Romans 8:35 "*Who shall separate us from the love of Christ? Shall trouble or hardship or persecution or famine or nakedness or danger or sword?*"

New International Version

Romans 8:37-39, "*No in all these things, we are more than conquerors through him who loved us. For I am convinced that neither death nor life, neither angels or demons, neither the present nor the future, nor any powers, neither height or depth, nor anything else in all creation, will be able to separate us for the love of God that in is in Christ Jesus*".

New International Version

Believers in Jesus Christ are called "conquerors". Jesus has already given you victory over your life. Pray this time of devotion would build your faith and draw you closer into a real and tangible relationship with Jesus. To know Jesus is to trust Him.

Psalm 9:10 *"Those who know Your name will trust in you, for you, Lord, have never forsaken those who seek you".*

New International Version

Questions

1. Have you prayed to receive Jesus Christ as your Savior?

2. Do you believe your faith in Jesus can help you through a crisis?

3. Have you considered how you can claim victory over your situation?

Prayer

Lord Jesus, I confess I am a sinner in need of Your abundant grace. I believe You died to forgive my sin and to offer eternal life. I pray to receive You as my personal Lord and savior. I give my life and circumstances to You. I pray to receive Your grace and to know you personally. Please give me strength as I walk this difficult road.

A Perfect Storm

Devotion 2

2 John 16:33

"I have told you these things, so that in me you may have peace. In this world, you will have trouble. But take heart! I have overcome the world".

New International Version

I live in a place where thunderstorms roll in and out faster than the time it takes to watch your favorite episode. In springtime and summer, heavy winds and tornadoes are commonplace. Every year there are homes and towns that incur devastation caused by colliding winds clashing together with forces so powerful they leave a wake of destruction. Some people live in climates that would chill the rest of us to the bone, while others choose to live in warmer temperatures where they face hurricanes and flooding. Regardless of what climate you live in, nature has a way of combining elements that come together at just the right time to cause damage. Equally as devastating are the tidal waves and dark clouds of life's difficulties that often blow in and catch us by surprise. Life sometimes has a way of dealing us a bad hand when we are already down or striking us at a time when we are already drowning. All at once, life can issue a series of problems that come together at the same time and cause us to feel the burden is too heavy to carry, as if we are in *A Perfect Storm*.

My family was caught in this type of force. Out of the blue, with no preexisting conditions, we found ourselves a thousand miles away from home in a *Pediatric Intensive Care Unit* with our baby girl. For three days the

4

team of pediatric doctors performed a series of tests to find out why Adalee had suffered a stroke. After reviewing her veins, blood, and heart the doctors could not find the reason of her "acute situation" but ruled that her stroke was caused by *"A Perfect Storm"*. For this to occur there were a handful of sources that had to come together in just the right way, and at just the right time, to result in this life-threatening situation. We were told that not finding the origin is good, and so much better than having a disease or problem with a major organ. We learned to take this as good news, yet Adalee's little body was still left debilitated. The wake of destruction left its damage.

Application

We all can relate to what it feels like when life delivers unwelcome difficulties to our doorsteps. Life is filled with hardships. Many of us live with physical ailments, health issues, or may suffer from pain or affliction of one kind or another. Some of us end up facing emergencies or life-threatening issues we hope we never have to encounter. We all have been impacted by the sickness of a loved one, or the death of a beloved friend or family member. Life can be hard, and we know there are going to be difficulties. Anticipating problems can cause us to feel the weight of the unknown cripple us with fear. If we allow it to creep in and overtake us it can cause us to live in fear of what is to come.The truth is we do not have to live dreading the unknown. Yes, this world is filled with brokenness, sickness, and eventually death, but we do not have to brace ourselves as if we are on a roller coaster with no harness. We do not have to live in misery or wallow in it. There is more hope than there is pain, and we can declare victory over defeat. If you do not already know, there is a God who loves you, who wants to comfort you, bring you peace, and lift you up not only when you are in your worst nightmare, but all the time. God wants a relationship with you and wants us to experience how real and tangible He is in our lives. John 16:33 tells us Jesus has already *"overcome the world."* His death on the cross and resurrection has given us all victory over death. When the perfect storm seems to swallow you and take over your life there is peace and comfort found in Jesus Christ.

1 Corinthians 15: 55-56 *"Where, O death is your victory? Where, O death is your sting? The sting of death is sin, and the power of sin is the law. But thanks be to God! He gives us the victory through our Lord Jesus Christ."*

Matthew 11:28 *"Come to me, all you who are weary and burdened, and I will give you rest".*

New International Version

Questions

1. Has your life been hit by *"A Perfect Storm"*?

2. Has the crisis in your life left destruction and feelings of defeat?

3. Do you believe God will give you strength to endure hardship?

Prayer

Lord Jesus, thank You for Your promise to give us hope and peace during the storms and difficulties in life. Help me to trust You, feel Your peace, and place my faith in You. Give me strength to endure this time, and to place hope in Your love and promise.

God Never Leaves Us

Devotion 3

Deuteronomy 31:6

"Be strong and courageous. Do not be afraid or terrified because of them, for the LORD your God goes with you; "He will never leave you nor forsake you."

New International Version

O n the morning of Wednesday, February 26, 2014, I immediately noticed a difference in our two-year old daughter. Something was not right, and the alarms of motherly intuition were sounding off and on high alert. Our joyful, chatty toddler was quiet, and one side of her mouth was not moving. By 3:30 p.m. that afternoon these small changes seemed even more apparent when I noticed her right leg dipping as she walked. After a quick call to our pediatrician's office back home, we rushed Adalee to the emergency room at *Intermountain Primary Children's Hospital* in Salt Lake City. In a matter of minutes, the doctors evaluated Adalee's symptoms. The *Pediatric ER* doctor looked at me and said *"I am worried about your daughter. I think she is having a stroke".* Immediately, doctors and nurses flooded the room and began drawing blood, poking Adalee for IVs, and prepping her for a *CAT* scan. It was apparent Adalee's brain had been affected and her ability to talk had been impaired while the other symptoms were progressing. Adalee was losing the ability to use the entire right side of her body, as well as her ability to speak. The doctors informed us the symptoms would worsen within the next thirty-six hours before she was stabilized. The next step was to answer a multitude of questions as to what caused our two-year-old to have a stroke. In the middle of the whirlwind, I stood in the *Emergency Room* hallway looking into a dark, empty corridor. Moments earlier, my daughter had been lying on the bed in the room adjacent to where I was standing. The team of doctors had whisked her away. I could hear my husband, Mark, and the doctor talking in the room next to me. My heart felt like a heavy bowling ball pressing down on my chest, and my stomach was a ball of knots pulling in opposite directions. Time. Stood. Still. In that moment, I felt the Holy Spirit fall over me as I heard a voice over my head state the word of God. I heard the Lord say to me,

"I will never leave you, nor forsake you.
"Sarah, I am here, I am God, and I. Am. Constant".

God's presence washed over me. It was as if He draped a cloak over my shoulders and I could feel the peace adorn my neck. The overwhelming sense of peace rested upon the anxiety in my stomach, and it calmed me. It did not make the ball of stress in my stomach go away, but it did compose my emotions. In that instant, the Lord spoke and prompted me He was there. The Lord used His own words from scripture and reminded me of His promise. He will always be with us and will never leave us.

God's word never says we will not endure hardship, tragedy, or loss. However, we can rest assured that when we experience pain and difficulties, He will always be there to give us strength, and HE DID! It felt the presence of God and He made Himself known to me. He spoke within my spirit, and He gave me peace to be able to handle the situation. The peace enabled me to process the loads of information we sifted through each time we spoke with the doctors, keep a clear mind to make the best decisions for Adalee, and to be emotionally strong for our daughter. God comforted me just like Mark and I wanted to comfort our sweet baby daughter. Even though it was just a moment, the Lord breathed through me several lessons with great depth and meaning that I would use to deal with this crisis and carry with me forever.

Application

God promises to always be there for us. God reveals Himself to us because He loves us and wants us to experience the comfort He alone can give in times of pain and crisis. There are many ways the Lord reveals Himself. God reveals Himself through scripture, prayer, the Holy Spirit, circumstances, and people. At the same time, the Holy Spirit will always work in accordance with scripture. God will never reveal Himself in a way that does not align with His word. If you are enduring a crisis, ask the Lord to open your heart and allow Him to reveal Himself to you. Pray the Lord will open your eyes, ears, and heart so that you can recognize His presence, His voice, and His love. Choose to believe He loves you and is there for you. It does not matter what you have done, or where you have been. He will always meet you where you are. Look at the number of times God has promised in scripture He will never leave us.

Deuteronomy 31:8 *"The LORD himself goes before you and will be with you; He will never leave you nor forsake you. "Do not be afraid; do not be discouraged."*

Joshua 1:9 *"Have I not commanded you? Be strong and courageous. Do not be terrified; do not be discouraged, for the Lord your God will be with you wherever you go."*

Hebrews 13:5 *"Keep your lives free from the love of money and be content with what you have, because God has said, "Never will I leave you; never will I forsake you."*

New International Version

9

Questions

1. Is there a reason it would be hard for you to believe that God wants to be there for you?

2. Do you feel peace in your life and how has that helped you during this time?

3. How has the Lord revealed Himself to you?

Prayer

Lord Jesus, thank You for Your promise to always be there for us. Draw close and help me to identify and experience Your presence. Open my eyes, ears, and heart to know how You are revealing Yourself to me.

Eternal Hope

Devotion 4

Romans 15:13
"May the God of hope fill you with all joy and peace in believing, so that by the power of the Holy Spirit you may abound in hope."
New International Version

T hings can change in an instant. The morning of February 26th, my sweet, bubbly, singing, dancing, life of the party, two–year-old was not her normal self. My baby changed overnight. In a raging instant, our lives changed, and our family of five had been turned upside down. All we knew was that our daughter's life, our lives, might never be the same. We were told she may NEVER be the same. Our daughter's normalcy was being stripped away. Her abilities, her personality, and her words were deteriorating before our eyes. Without warning the rug of normality was pulled out from beneath our feet. The existence of our "normal" vanished, and for weeks we did not know if Adalee would ever be the same. We did not know if Adalee would ever walk or talk again. We did not know if she would be in a wheelchair for the rest of her life, or if we were going to have to learn sign language since she lost her ability to communicate with words. The doctors could not give concrete answers. We were told that children have a good chance at recovery, but the team of neurologists could not offer any guarantees. The words God spoke to me were replaying in my mind

"I am here. I am God, and I am Constant".

The phrase offered an eternal perspective that gave me a glimpse of a bigger picture. I felt hope in life beyond this earth. Adalee's little body was broken, but my heart rested on a hope that gives us assurance that God will never change, and that one day she would be whole again in eternity. We were reminded how this life is so very temporary. Our material possessions and physical abilities here on earth cannot be measured against an eternity with God.

Application

Those who have endured a similar situation might never be the same on this earth but can someday be restored in eternity with Jesus Christ. To have an eternal perspective we must believe that Jesus is Lord and accept Him as our Savior. Eternal peace comes from knowing that no matter what happens here on earth we will live with Jesus in eternity. This world is ever changing, and we are constantly reminded that the only thing in life that is constant, other than God, is change. We must be ready. We do not have to live in fear, but we must be prepared for our eternal future. If you have endured physical loss or hardship rest assured, you will one day be whole again. Ask the Lord to give you an eternal perspective to see beyond this earthly realm.

2 Corinthians 4:17-18 *"For our light and momentary troubles are achieving for us an eternal glory that far outweighs them all. So we fix our eyes not on what is seen, but what is unseen, since what is seen is temporary, but what is unseen is eternal".*
New International Version

Questions

1. Has your life instantly changed and your "normal" turned upside down?

2. How often do you think in terms of your eternal future?

3. Do you see how your daily life and situations have eternal impact?

Prayer

Lord Jesus, thank You for giving me eternal life through Your sacrifice and resurrection. Give me an eternal perspective in my daily life, and as I walk through difficulty. Help me to better understand my current situation, and how I can view it from an eternal perspective.

Perspective Is Grounding

Devotion 5

Psalm 103:2-4

"Bless the Lord, O my soul, and forget none of His benefits; Who pardons all your iniquities; Who heals all your diseases; Who redeems your life from the pit, who crowns you with loving-kindness and compassion...".

New International Version

Adalee had to go under anesthesia for her *MRI*. Once she was awake, a team of nurses wheeled her from the recovery room to the *Pediatric Intensive Care Unit (PICU)*. The room in the *PICU* was very small and had only three walls. The fourth wall was a curtain, and there was little space and privacy. By the time we got Adalee settled she fell asleep around 3:00 a.m. I laid down to try and get some rest, but the sights and sounds of the *PICU* were mentally and emotionally excruciating. On the other side of the curtain, I heard a newborn baby with *Respiratory Syncytial Virus*, and the sounds this sick newborn made as it coughed will forever be embedded in my brain. It was awful and hands down, one of the worst sounds I have ever heard. It took everything I had not to power through the curtain and tend to the tiny infant curled up on its stomach. I knew acting out on that motherly impulse would violate all kinds of hospital rules, so I chose to be rational and only peeked at the infant through the curtain. At the same time, across the hall there was a room with glass walls and an open door where I could see what appeared to be a boy around the age of 12 who was in a coma.

Hours earlier when we entered the *PICU,* I noticed that behind the glass walls a group of doctors and nurses surrounded the bed side as they conducted some type of procedure. Hours later when I finally sat down, the procedure had ended, and the parents and family members laid on the chairs next to their son's bedside. From moment to moment they would sleep, pace, and watch over him in hopes he would wake. I watched the scenario play out and still had room in my aching stomach to feel the agony these parents endured. As one parent to another, it was heart wrenching to have a small portion of an idea of what they were experiencing. In these surroundings the Lord ministered to me again and gave me perspective. At least my daughter had been awake and had come out of her anesthesia. I knew Adalee was not going to die, or at least the thought had not occurred to me. Her circumstances were life threatening and completely unknown, but she was alive and had been aware of what was going on around her. Adalee may have been confused, but I could hold her, and she received comfort from my arms. In those moments God gave me perspective, and perspective is grounding. Adalee was in a very serious state and would have lifelong issues and challenges based on what we knew from the last few hours, but I was not losing her. I was so thankful that her very serious condition was not worse. This perspective also made me feel humble and grateful that she was alive, and it offered me a sense of responsibility to pray for the boy across the hall, his family, and the baby next to us. I have prayed for the boy and his family since we left the *PICU.* During the next two and half days while Adalee was a patient in the *PICU* he did not wake. My heart will always feel pain for his parents, and when I feel it, I pray for them.

Application

A healthy perspective keeps us grounded and able to see ourselves and our situations through a wider lens. Even in our own dire circumstances there are always others who are experiencing pain beyond what we bear. Perspective is a gift and with it comes a responsibility. It allows us to find reasons to be thankful even when life is hard to handle. It also reminds us to look beyond ourselves and to remember others who are hurting. It is so easy to be self-consumed when dealing with pain. Perspective allows us to look outward into the lives of people around us, and to remember we can use our own hardships to pray and minister to others. There is always something for which we can be thankful. Finding ways to be thankful changes our heart, minds, and outlook.

1 Thessalonians 5:16-18

"Be joyful always; pray continually; give thanks in all circumstances, for this is God's will for you in Christ Jesus."

New International Version

Questions

1. How would a healthy perspective benefit you as you deal with \
your own pain?

2. When you are dealing with your own circumstance do you notice others who are suffering or dealing with difficulty?

3. In what ways would perspective help you identify the blessings in your life?

Prayer

Lord, I thank You for the blessings in my life. When I am dealing with difficulty and pain help me to remember the good things You have given me. Please give me perspective and help me remember to pray for others who are also dealing with pain.

A Call to Action

Philippians 4:6-7

"**D**o not be anxious about anything, but in everything, by prayer and petition, with thanksgiving, present your requests to God, which transcends understanding, will guard your hearts and your minds in Christ Jesus."

New International Version

The next morning, I woke up just before 6:00 a.m. as nurses attended to Adalee. The *Pediatric Intensive Care Unit* began to buzz as teams of residents and doctors began their rounds. It was clear Adalee was unable to use her right arm and leg. The right side of her face was drooping, she did not speak, and only cried when the nurse drew her blood. After speaking to the team of pediatric neurologists, I began to put together a clearer picture of Adalee's situation. I learned every stroke and patient recovery is different. The neurologists made it very clear they could not predict if Adalee would recover her ability to speak or use the right side of her body. The doctors said she "could" recover up to 80% of what she lost, but that a full recovery was not possible. At the same time, the doctors were optimistic she could recover some of her abilities. As a young child her brain had the potential to rewire itself around what is referred to as the "dead spot". However, the neurologists told me she would not be able to regain 100% of the abilities she lost. The reality we faced was Adalee may never walk or run again. After we waded our way through the daily assessments, discussions, and questions, I found a moment alone at Adalee's bedside. I stood and closed my eyes and prayed. I said, *"Lord, I know you have the power to heal Adalee 100%. I pray You would heal her so she can have a full recovery. Lord, I pray Adalee would live a normal life. I pray she would walk, talk, and Lord I pray she will RUN!"*. As I prayed the prayer, I offered it to the Lord and placed it is His hands. My faith was strong, but I also understood not every prayer ends the way we want. I handed it over the to the Lord, so I could focus on this new reality and best prepare for what was ahead. I had a lot of work to do to care for my child. Next, as humbly as I could, I called on my family, church, and community to pray. I took a picture of Adalee and posted it to my social media page and asked my family in faith to pray the same prayer. I did not realize it then, but my post that day turned into a call to action for our family, friends, and our church home. It was a hand off and they stood in the gap for us.

Application

God did not create us to live life alone. We need a community of people to thrive on ordinary days, as well as to support us through difficult seasons. It is a tremendous blessing to have people in our lives that will pray with us and for us. Never be ashamed to ask those you trust to pray for you. Often, the burden is too heavy to carry alone. Many times, we desperately need the support of prayer as we deal with the details of our circumstances. Remember to look for opportunities to pray for others. There is always someone who needs prayer.

Galatians 6:2 *"Carry each other's burdens, and in this way, you will fulfill the law of Christ."*

Matthew 21:22 *"If you believe, you will receive whatever you ask for in prayer."*

New International Version

If you feel alone and do not know someone who can pray for you ask God to send someone into your life that believes in the power of prayer. Attend or reach out to a local church or ministry that is Christ focused.

Questions

1. Have you released your situation to the Lord in prayer?

2. Do you have someone to pray for you during this time?

3. What action can you take to pray for others?

Prayer

Lord Jesus, I have faith You can do anything. Your scriptures proclaim Your power and majesty. I pray You will demonstrate Your glory in my circumstances. I pray You would send me a community of faith to support me in prayer. May I see You working in every detail. Open my eyes to see how I can also stand in the gap and pray for others.

God Is Our Refuge

Devotion 7

Psalm 46:1-3

"God is our refuge and strength, an ever-present help in trouble. Therefore, we will not fear, though the earth gives way and the mountains fall into the heart of the sea, though its waters roar and foam and the mountains quake with their surging."

New International Version

Friday morning came quickly, and I was able to get Adalee down for a nap in the *Pediatric Intensive Care Unit*. Mark brought me a change of clothes and my toiletry bag so I could shower at the hospital while Adalee slept. Having a shower and putting on fresh clothes with comfortable shoes felt cozy. Mark insisted I eat since I had not had any food in 36 hours. The bowling ball of stress had repressed hunger pains and I could not stomach any food, but I finally agreed. That afternoon Adalee was considered stable, and the order was given that she be released from the *PICU* to be moved to a regular room. We were relieved her little body had overcome this hurtle. During Adalee's afternoon nap Mark and I went down to the cafeteria to eat. By this time, I was very hungry and ordered a large, juicy hamburger with all the trimmings. We sat down at a table for two, faced one another, and prayed. Mark thanked the Lord that Adalee was stable enough to be transferred to a regular room. As I opened my eyes a feeling of immense relief rushed over me, and as I took the first bite of my burger, I felt big crocodile tears pour out of my eyes and down my face. It was the first time I thought about my own emotions. I began to repeat *"Thank you Lord"*, over and over. Those tears symbolized the tidal wave of relief in my spirit and body. Mark sat there being strong. His eyes reflected emotion as well, but he chose to be a force of strength. He was steady, and God gave him the ability to be there for me which gave me comfort. The truth was we both felt the Lord's strength sustain us. Our little world had been shaken to its core, and we were in the middle of a crisis parents hope to never endure. There was tremendous relief our daughter had stabilized, but her future was unknown. Yet we felt the Lord's strength sustain us and we were not fearful. I recognized the Lord's strength in my husband's eyes. I felt as if I was being held up by God's hand as the scripture promises.

Isaiah 41:10 *"Fear not, for I am with you; be not dismayed, for I am your God; I will strengthen you, I will help you, I will uphold you with my righteous right hand."*

English Standard Version

Application

The word "refuge" means to seek protection from danger or trouble. When we are facing distress, or difficult circumstances, we can find refuge in God. The scripture says the *"earth will give way"* and *"the mountains will fall into the sea"*. In other words, our physical realm will not always be secure. Our health, our material possessions, and our earthly life will fade and often face trouble. At the same time, Psalm 46 says the Lord is our *"ever-present help"* in the scariest circumstances. We do not have to be fearful when the God of the universe is there to give us protection. We can believe and count on the written words in the bible. We begin by exercising our faith, asking through prayer, and in turn can receive a supernatural strength. Our physical and earthly circumstances may still be chaotic, but God's refuge is a stronghold that will offer peace to help us get through the difficulty. God holds us in His hands.

Questions

1. When you think of the word "refuge" what comes to mind?

2. Have you taken refuge in God's promise?

3. How has God given you strength in your time of need?

Prayer

Lord, thank You for helping us when we face trouble. The storms of life are overwhelming. I desire to take refuge in Your presence. Please protect me from any physical or spiritual elements that may seem dangerous or out of control. Allow me to recognize Your presence. Sustain me with Your strength during this difficult time.

Step-By-Step

Devotion 8

Psalm 62:1-2

"Truly my soul finds rest in God; my salvation comes from him. Truly he is my
rock and my salvation; He is my fortress; I will never be shaken."

New International Version

By late Friday afternoon Adalee was settled into her new hospital room. Monitors and chords were removed from her body, but her IVs remained. We began to consult with additional teams of doctors and therapists to discuss the process of rehabilitation. Adalee would begin a new round of tests to see if she could swallow liquids without coughing or choking. The goal was to strengthen the muscles in her mouth and throat so she could eat and hopefully speak again. Our time was filled talking with multiple groups of doctors, making decisions, scheduling therapies, running tests, discussing results, and looking ahead to the next step. We were slowly wading through progress. We could see Adalee's cognitive ability, and she was able to understand our communication. Adalee could follow commands, point to objects in books, held up her fingers on her left hand as if she was counting, and we were communicating even though she was not talking. Every moment of progress was an answered prayer. We were taking it step by step. Once again, we did not know what life would look like moving forward, but we found rest in our eternal assurances. Our faith provided a bedrock of eternal security, and our souls rested on God's promises.

Application

Many times, we must walk through hard situations one step at a time. In some cases, there may be an instant solution. Other times patience is required as progress seems to happen slowly. The theme of Psalm 62 is to place hope in God. We must believe He is in control and wait patiently on Him. Our relief comes through eternal salvation, which offers hope and security.

Psalm 62 verse 8 says *"Then I will ever sing praise to your name and fulfill my vows day after day."* Verse 8 reminds us to be committed to praising God through the good and difficult times. The journey may not be easy, but in every step, we can praise God and our hearts will be lifted-up to help us put one foot in front of the other.

Questions

1. Are you able to push forward taking one step at a time?

2. Is anything preventing you from progressing through your circumstances?

3. Are you fearful? If so, how can trusting in God help you take the next step?

Prayer

Lord, thank You for Your promise of hope. There are days where it is difficult to put one foot in front of the other. Help my soul find rest in Your promise of eternal salvation. Give me the strength to move forward step by step.

Love

1 Corinthians 13:13

"And now these three remain: faith, hope, and love. But the greatest of these is love".

New International Version

Friday evening Mark brought our seven-year-old son, Seth, and our five-year-old daughter, Hannah Grace to the hospital to visit. It had been several days since I had seen them. It was so good to put my arms around them and give them hugs. Their presence was great medicine for Adalee. While Adalee took a nap in her hospital room, the four of us were able to go down to the cafeteria and eat dinner as a family. It brought us joy to get to hear about their ski school and how they had been having a great time with cousins. Mark had done a superior job at juggling their schedule during the day, so they did not feel the weight of the situation. We were thankful they had been able to stay with family. During dinner, we spoke openly and directly with them about Adalee to help them understand her condition. Afterward, we all went back to Adalee's room to share time together. It gave Adalee a sense of normalcy to be around her big brother and sister. The time together was one of the most precious times we have experienced as a family. The kids were so sweet and encouraging to their little sister, and I was so proud of them. Not once did they gasp at the IVs or get upset by the hospital equipment. They simply were excited to see her and instantly acclimated to her changes. Seth and Hannah Grace took turns pushing her in a child's wheelchair down the hallway pointing to all the colorful, kid friendly murals painted on the walls of the children's hospital. I was able to capture the moment on video and took a picture of Mark and the kids surrounding Adalee as she sat in her wheelchair. Adalee was smiling from the left side of her mouth, so happy to be with all of us. I could see she was trying hard to pose for the camera even though half of her face would not move. That night my heart was full of joy to see my precious family in action, loving on one another, and being together for the first time after a life-threatening crisis. My children smiled, played, laughed, and I thanked the Lord for such a blessing. I was uplifted and knew in that moment that no matter Adalee's condition her siblings would accept her for who she was. It was one of the most rewarding moment's I have had as a parent. Mark and I were touched by how God showed His love through our small children. We were blessed immeasurably.

Application

God's unconditional love overlooks our inabilities and appearances, and accepts us when we are broken, hurting, and lifts us up to feel supernatural strength. There is immense power in love, yet it can be felt in the smallest gestures. It can bring us to our knees and soften the hardest heart. Love can bridge deep divides, heal wounds, conquer heartache, and minister in sorrowful circumstances. God wants us to feel His love in the deepest and most tender ways when we are dealing with a crisis. God can also show us His infinite love through people, even small children, or through a situation. We can be thankful for those God places in our lives who love us unconditionally. We can also choose to reach out beyond our difficulty and love others. We can pray God will show us how to love others in a way that reflects His character.

Questions

1. How has God shown you love during your crisis?

2. Have you expressed thankfulness for the people in your life that love you unconditionally?

3. Have you told them they are a blessing to you?

4. How do you think it would help you to reach beyond your difficulty to extend love to someone in need?

Prayer

Lord, thankful for Your unconditional love. Thank You for the blessing of people in my life who show me love. Help me to also show love to others. May the power of Your love continue to shape me, and change hearts and lives around me.

Army of Prayer of Warriors

Devotion 10

Matthew 18:20

"For where two or three come together in my name, there I am with them."

New International Version

As the weekend approached, we received messages, voicemails, emails, and texts, from many of our friends and family. The only phone calls we had time to make were to our parents. I did not have time to reply or give individual updates on Adalee' progress. Our loved ones understood and still made it a point to let us know our family, church, and friends were praying for Adalee. The staff and members at our church spent time praying for Adalee in meetings, choir rehearsals, Sunday morning classes, and bible studies. They called on the Lord to offer our daughter healing. Adalee attended a *Mother's Day Out* program at our church. When the teachers and staff heard the news that Adalee had suffered a stroke, they stayed after hours and took time out of their day to gather in a circle, hold hands, and pray for our family. Our parents called on their churches, bible studies, and prayer chains to begin praying. Our extended family and friends did the same. Word spread quickly. In a few days we witnessed my initial social media post turn into a platform of prayer. We witnessed a prayer chain turn into an *Army of Prayer Warriors* that began in Texas and ended up reaching across the country from the northeast to Indiana, Illinois, and California. We were humbled that total strangers from bible studies and churches across the nation would pray over our child. It was a powerful force to be on the receiving end. Mark and I were humbled by the care and concern we received. We did not realize until later how many people prayed over Adalee, for Seth and Hannah Grace, and for Mark and me. However, we can tell you we felt the prayers. We felt the Lords strength sustain us. It is an incredible sensation to feel lifted-up in prayer, and to feel strength from the prayers of people you do not even know. We felt the Lord's power but had no idea how those prayers would capture our attention in the coming days.

Psalm 29: 11 *"The Lord gives strength to His people; the Lord blesses His people with peace".*

Mark 11:24 *"Therefore I tell you, whatever you ask in prayer, believe that you have received it, and it will be yours."*
New International Version

Application

It is a tremendous blessing to receive prayer from others, and incredible to watch a community of believers turn into an *Army of Prayer Warriors.* There is power in prayer, and we can pray with authority. Matthew 18:20 tell us there is incredible power when two or more believers pray according to God's will.

Ephesians 6:18 *"And pray in the spirit on all occasions with all kinds of requests. With this in mind be alert and always keep praying for all the saints."*
New International Version

If you are blessed with a Christian community, never be afraid to ask for prayer. Take the opportunity to pray for others. Many times, praying for others builds our faith just as much, if not more, than the person for which we are praying. If you do not know someone you can trust to pray for you ask the Lord to bring a community of Christ followers into your life. Seek out a church and ask God to lead you to the right place.

Questions

1. Have you made prayer a priority as you walk through your crisis?

2. Have you experienced the power of prayer when two or more people are gathered and praying together?

3. How can praying with others build your faith?

Prayer

Lord, thank You that we can pray to you. Thank You for listening and allowing us to pour out our hearts and lay our requests before You. Help me to grow in my prayer life. Help me to pray according to Your will and see Your answered prayer in my life. Grant me the opportunity to experience the blessing of praying with others. Lord, please give me the opportunity to be a part of a group that lifts people up in moments of crisis and to see Your power when praying together.

God's Purpose

Devotion 11

Jeremiah 29:11

"For I know the plans I have for you", declares the Lord, "plans to prosper you and not to harm you, plans to give you a hope and a future."

New International Version

I could sense the Lord holding me up and giving me the ability to focus and deal with the situation in a steady manner. We had already received good news with every test result, and I began to feel the responsibility of letting everyone know how their prayers were making a difference for Adalee, as well as for the rest of the family. To keep everyone up to date on Adalee's progress I started a *Caring Bridge* blog. Mark and I did not have time to respond to every person who left us messages, and a blog was a tool to help us reach everyone. It allowed us to ask for specific prayers, as well as share about the answered prayer we already witnessed through Adalee's improvement. I felt the Lord impress upon my spirit to write about how He was revealing Himself and ministering to us. Once I began posting blogs updates, we received messages from friends who shared how God was building their faith through praying for our family and reading about Adalee's progress. As we began to hear how Adalee's crisis was impacting the faith of others, Mark offered some insightful words, *"We do not know why this happened, but it may not be about us."* Mark catapulted our faith to the next level. He was pointing out there may be a bigger picture we cannot see. We do not know why bad things happen, but we do know God can use it for His glory. Jeremiah 29:11 promises God has a purpose for our lives.

Isaiah 43:7 says, *"everyone who is called by my name, who I created for my glory, who I formed and made."*

New International Version

I grappled with the notion that our purpose is to glorify God. Adalee's life was made to glorify Him, and He made her with a purpose. I may not understand or have all the answers as to why this happened, or why there was an entire hospital of sick and suffering children. I am not big enough, smart enough, or spiritual enough to see the whole picture. I am reminded that is why it is called "faith". I do not believe God wanted my daughter to have a stroke but trust He can use our suffering to achieve His plan and purpose.

Application

It can be difficult to try and make sense of our pain. Sometimes there are no clear answers. We know that when we suffer God says he will sustain us. Jeremiah 29:11 tells us God wants us to prosper and that He does not want harm to come to us. We can rest assured His word is true because Luke 1:37 tells us *"For no word from God will ever fail".* We also know we live in a fallen world where sin dwells and our bodies are imperfect. We get to make the choice to trust in the Lord and not rely on our own understanding of how our circumstances will play out in this earthly realm. Our vantage point is much smaller than the creator of the universe.

Isaiah 55:8-9 *"For my thoughts are not your thoughts, neither are your ways my ways," declares the Lord. "As the heavens are higher than the earth, so are my ways higher than your ways and my thoughts than your thoughts."*

New International Version

God can turn our bleak circumstances into a purposeful testimony of His faithfulness, use it to build our own faith, and the faith of others. Either way, we can offer a willing heart to trust Him even in the hardest circumstances.

Trusting in the Lord means coming to terms with the fact we may not be able to see the big picture. Many times, we may never fully understand it this side of eternity. What He makes very clear to us is that He will give us strength.

Proverbs 3:5 -6 *"Trust in the LORD with all your heart; do not depend on your own understanding. Seek his will in all you do, and he will show you which path to take."*

New International Version

It is through the process of experiencing God's strength and developing trust that our faith grows stronger. We can literally place our trust in the hands of God.

Questions

1. When you think of God's plan for your life what comes to mind?

2. How has the Lord taken your suffering and used it for good?

3. Have you considered your suffering could make an eternal impact on someone else?

4. What testimony of faith do you see God creating from your story?

Prayer

Lord, thank You for the plans and purpose You have for my life. Help me to see how You can take my difficulty and bring about something beautiful and good. Help me to trust in You even though I may not fully understand how You are working in my life, or the lives of others around me. I stand on the promise of hope and purpose for my life. May you see me through to Your glorious conclusion.

Ups and Downs

Devotion 12

Isaiah 40:29-31

"He gives strength to the weary and increases the power of the weak. Even youths grow tired and weary, but those who hope in the Lord will renew their strength. They will soar on wings like. eagles; they will run and not grow weary; they will walk and not be faint."

New International Version

The following days in the hospital were met with ups and downs. Adalee faced setbacks and made improvements. Adalee and I both came down with head colds and her room was placed on quarantine. It was the seventh day into our hospital stay and I was physically and emotionally spent. The weight of our crisis and realization of the long-term aftermath was settling in. I was riding on little sleep, and the setbacks were draining. Our emotions and reality were swinging back and forth on a pendulum. Relief and concern felt like a heavy ocean wave pulling us back and forth. It was as if I were wading in water that was too strong for swimming.

On that seventh morning, I woke before dawn. I slipped down to the cafeteria for some strong coffee. While standing in line, I noticed a lady standing next to me. The look on her face spoke of distress, and she was exhausted. It was a look I replicated and easily understood. We were both hovering over the coffee machine, tired and looking for a pick me up, when she asked me how long I had been at the hospital. When I replied, *"it is my seventh day"*, she told me she had been there two weeks. It was a sobering reminder that there were children and families who were staying at the children's hospital for longer than I would experience. Days, weeks, months …. much longer. Emotions ran deep and were difficult to process. I sipped my coffee and walked through the hollow hallways back to Adalee's room. I saw faces of parents and children in similar situations. I was acutely aware and beyond grateful that I knew my child would live. I did not know if Adalee would ever walk or talk again, but I knew she was alive and had some type of future. The feeling of sober relief was consuming. At the same time, I was hit in the stomach with sorrow I felt for families I passed on the oncology and neurology floor. I felt immense grief balanced with my own relief, gratefulness, thankfulness, humbleness, and heartache for the unknown. Each day we were dealing with a level of grief, but feelings of hope grew into reality as we could see Adalee's progress. I would wear these feelings like a necklace every day for the next few weeks and months. This was one of the times where the Lord offered me strength as He kept my mind in check.

Application

Heartache takes a tremendous toll on our human bodies, minds, and spirits. Navigating through the haze of mixed emotions and physical turmoil can leave us feeling weak and depleted. When life crashes in and seems to be more than we can bear, we can ask the Lord for strength. God promises to "renew" our strength. Our weary souls can soar on his mighty breath that lifts us up and allows us to experience what it means for God to carry us. Life is always met with ups and downs. During our challenges we can place hope in God and know His promise of strength will help us overcome difficulty.

Questions

1. How have you dealt with the ups and downs of your
   circumstances?

2. Are you able to ask the Lord to renew your strength? If not, what is holding you back?

3. If you have felt the Lord, bring His radiant life to your weary bones explain how it impacts you.

Prayer

Lord, thank You for describing a beautiful picture of how You carry us. I place my hope in You. Please "renew" my strength to get me through this hardship. I pray Your spirit will draw close and I will be able to see how You are working in my life.

Moving Forward

Devotion 13

Romans 12:12
"Be joyful in hope, patient in affliction, faithful in prayer."

New International Version

A dalee continued to make progress. She began to eat and drink on her own, her IVs were taken out of her little body, and she could sit up and play with *Barbies* with one hand on the floor. Plans were set in motion to fly home to Texas, and the doctors laid out a plan for in-patient and out-patient therapy. It was time to begin the process of moving forward. Adalee had overcome the life-threatening stages of brain trauma, but our journey was just beginning. The pediatric specialists informed us Adalee would undergo at least two and a half years of speech, occupational, and physical therapy. To hear the road ahead was going to take years was startling, but for our daughter to improve and to help our other children live as normal a life as possible, we forged ahead. We made a choice to praise God for his answered prayer, found hope through the blessing of our faith and family, and realized this process was going to require a lot of patience. Having faith helped us to grasp what we were dealing with and then look ahead to know how to handle it. It helped us to move forward.

Application

Moving forward does not mean there will not be more challenges. In order to move forward we must make a choice. We can sit in our pain or push on. Pressing into the Lord will provide the strength needed to take the next step. Many times, during a crisis our faith can be tested, our patience worn thin. To combat the physical and mental strain we can pray for patience when afflicted, and in turn receive the joy in the eternal hope God promises. Our commitment to remaining faithful to prayer will help us remember the ways God has worked in our lives. Choosing to persist and move forward requires effort, but the process of persistent prayer creates discipline and perseverance.

James 1:2-3 says, *"Consider it pure joy, my brothers, whenever you face trials of many kinds, because you know that the testing of your faith develops perseverance."*
New International Version

The word "joy" in this verse does not mean we should feel happy about our trials. It means if we choose, we can find joy in the opportunity to develop a deeper relationship with the Lord. We cannot control our circumstances, but we can choose how we handle them. James 1:2-3 teaches us to look at the larger spiritual implication for our whole life and how it affects our spiritual journey.

Questions

1. How could you look beyond your current trial to see how it can impact your spiritual life as a whole?

2. Do you believe the opportunity to pursue a deeper walk with Christ is something worth rejoicing?

3. Dealing with pain and difficulty is so emotional. How can you give your emotion to the Lord?

Prayer

Lord, help me to move forward. Give me the strength to steadily persevere. Please give me patience during my affliction. May I receive the joy in experiencing You during these difficult moments.

Home

Devotion 14

Matthew 7:24-27

"Therefore, everyone who hears these words of mine and puts them into practice is like a wise man who built his house on the rock. 25 The rain came down, the streams rose, and the winds blew and beat against that house; yet it did not fall, because it had its foundation on the rock. 26 But everyone who hears these words of mine and does not put them into practice is like a foolish man who built his house on sand. 27 The rain came down, the streams rose, and the winds blew and beat against that house, and it fell with a great crash."

New International Version

Adalee continued to make progress. After nearly two weeks in the hospital Adalee was released to be transferred to a pediatric in-patient rehabilitation center in Dallas. Fortunately, she was stable enough to handle a commercial flight. This meant our family of five was able to go home. Plans were set in motion to fly home to Texas, and the doctors laid out a plan for in-patient and out-patient therapy. Adalee had overcome the life-threatening stages of brain trauma, but our journey was just beginning. We flew to Dallas where we had a layover before catching our connecting flight home to Waco. My family lives in Dallas so my parents, sister, and aunt met us at the airport during our layover. We met my family with hugs and felt relief to be with them. They expressed how helpless they felt being so far away while Adalee was in the hospital. The hearts of our parents had been heavily burdened, and it lifted all our spirits to feel at home in one another's presence. It was hard to watch them adjust to Adalee's condition as she was still not talking, walking, or moving the right side of her body. Yet our short time together was therapeutic. Our family of five took the flight home to Waco. Arriving home brought us comfort. At the same time, it was chaotic to get everyone settled, unpacked, and then prepare for another extended hospital stay for Adalee. Adalee and I had one night at home before we had to turn around and drive back to Dallas to check into the pediatric in-patient facility. Mark would stay at home in Waco with Seth and Hannah Grace, work his job, and handle my additional responsibilities for our businesses, parenting, and household.

Application

The presence of home offers familiarity and peace. The brick and mortar that provide us shelter can surely bring us comfort at the end of a long day or an extended vacation. Yet our actual "home" is where we build our foundation in Christ. We feel at home with family, friends, and loved ones but our spirit will feel true security that comes from Jesus Christ. Our physical home is symbolic of our faith. We can consider if our faith is rooted enough to withstand the "storms" we endure. We can choose to use a time of difficulty to water our roots with scripture and pray to strengthen the foundation of our faith. To continue to build our faith "on the rock" means to stand on God's promise of salvation that can never be shaken. We lay our roots when we receive Jesus as our Savior, and our foundation will grow strong when we are willing to listen, respond, and to obey as a Christ follower. If our faith is built on sand, it will not withstand a perfect storm. If we choose to seek wisdom in scripture our foundation can be strengthened. As we navigate treacherous circumstances, our response in faith can have a tremendous impact on our loved ones, and those who live under our roof. During a crisis it feels comforting to be home and around those we love, and we can consider how we build upon our spiritual foundation.

Questions

1. Where do you feel most at home?

2. Have you considered if your faith is built on a solid rock or sinking sand?

3. What are some ways you can work to strengthen your faith and home during this time?

4. How will your reaction and faith impact your loved ones?

Prayer

Lord, thank You for the ability to respond to You in praise and prayer. Strengthen my faith to be firmly grounded to withstand the storms I endure. May my faith be like the house that stood firmly on the rock. Thank you for my loved ones and the comfort provided by their presence. Watch over my loved ones, and may they find rest and peace in You.

God of Comfort

Devotion 15

2 Corinthians 1:3-4

"Praise be to the God and Father of our Lord Jesus Christ, the Father of compassion and the God of all comfort, 4 who comforts us in all our troubles, so that we can comfort those in any trouble with the comfort we ourselves receive from God."

New International Version

The doctors projected Adalee would be in in-patient therapy for a minimum of eight to twelve weeks. I would be staying with her in the pediatric rehabilitation hospital, which meant I had one night to pack any items we may need for several months. In the middle of our packing extravaganza, a sweet friend dropped off a gift that offered incredible comfort. Our friends had recently endured an extended stay at a pediatric hospital with their youngest daughter who had undergone open heart surgery. This couple knew what items we would need for a long hospital stay and brought them in a large, plastic bin. Inside were items I needed, but I had no idea I needed them. It was so helpful. Tucked inside was an extra soft blanket, a towel mat, towels, and wash clothes for the hospital bathroom. In addition, were a couple of plates and forks, snack items, extra toiletries, a journal, and a few toys for Adalee. As I thumbed through the empty pages of the journal, I found a sweet note written inside. My caring friend told me she knew I would need to write down the information that would be discussed with the doctors each day. Only someone who has been through a similar circumstance would know how to offer such comfort through items I did not even know I needed. Our friends knew how to make our stay more comfortable and provided a way to reach out and to minister to us.

I began to see ministry through a different lens. In many situations, the people who know how to minister the most are the ones who have been through similar experiences. The same evening an acquaintance whose child has a serious medical condition wrote me a note to welcome me to a "club". She wrote:

It was a club where you understood the depth of the feelings of the children and parents who were going through sickness. It was a club where we would understand the weariness and the fatigue that meant sitting up night after night as your child lay in a hospital bed while his or her future is unknown. A club where your child undergoes test after test to hopefully find a reason, cause, or treatment. At the same time, this understanding comes with the ability to relate, empathize, and find the right words to offer support. We would now understand how to love, help, and comfort others who unwillingly become members of this "club".

Her words of understanding were able to reach my heart in a special way. She understood what I was feeling. I did not grasp the whole picture but realized that evening our child's situation would change us forever. In the future, our family would know how to help and offer support to others in the same way.

Application

There are many ways God comforts us, and one way is through people. The Lord uses others to bring us comfort. Encouraging words, kind gestures, and acts of service are ways we empathize and offer understanding and love. Showing up for the people God lays on our hearts is a way He ministers to those in need. When we wade through the harsh elements of a crisis and receive comfort from others, it teaches us to know how to do the same. Our own crisis gives us experience and the ability to relate to someone who walks a similar road, and we can allow our difficulty to teach us how to help others. We can use our own experiences to pass along empathy and understanding of how to offer support. We have the choice to look inward into our own pain or loss, or we can look outward to those who are hurting. Making the choice to allow our adversity to equip us for ministry will open our eyes to how the Lord will use our situation for good and to bring Him glory.

Questions

1. How has God used people to bring you comfort?

2. What have you learned in your crisis that could offer comfort to someone in a similar situation?

3. How has your view of those around you changed due to your crisis?

Prayer

Lord, thank You that You are the God of all comfort. Thank You for using people to minister to us during difficult times. I pray to receive Your comfort, and that I will learn how to offer others the same comfort I have received from you. Show me ways to show support to people in my life.

Give Thanks

Devotion 16

1 Thessalonians 5:16-18
"Rejoice always, pray continually, give thanks in all circumstances; for this is God's will for you in Christ Jesus."

New International Version

I t was a quick turn-around. The next morning Mark and I assumed our roles. He would stay with Seth and Hannah Grace, work his job, and handle my responsibilities while I went to Dallas to stay with Adalee during in-patient rehabilitation. It was not easy leaving them, and we did not know for certain how long I would be gone. I was thankful for Mark's incredible ability to maintain our lives and children at home.

Less than two hours later Adalee and I arrived at *Our Children's House* which sat adjacent to downtown Dallas. Nestled across the street from *Baylor Medical Center*, the children's rehabilitation center was a facility built to make its residents feel as if they were at home. It was a charming Victorian style building with glowing stain glass windows and a round chapel. My parents met us there to help unload luggage, and when we arrived to Adalee's room we found it had been decorated with sweet pictures drawn by my nieces. Adalee's name decorated the wall in rainbow colors. My sister, Laura, and her three kids, had turned Adalee's bare, stark, room into a bright and cheerful residence. The girls found a way to paint color into our circumstances. Laura also gifted me some delicious coffee syrups so I could indulge in a tasty, warm, treat each morning. I enjoyed the decadent coffee, and each day I was reminded of her thoughtfulness. Adalee loved the attention from her grandparents and being around familiar faces helped her transition into another new place while dealing with the changes in her little body. The rest of the day was filled with doctor meetings and assessments. The team of pediatric physicians was wonderful, but Adalee sat in silence showing no signs of improvement in her speech. Evening approached and the bustle calmed down for the night. I placed Adalee in her hospital bed that was shaped like a giant, white, bird cage. The safety contraption looked confining but gave me comfort she would rest peacefully. After my parents left for the evening, I stood in the low lights of the hospital room. I walked over to the large, white pained window and took in the multi-colored lights of the familiar skyline. I realized I had the perfect view of downtown Dallas. As I stood looking out into the city that was my childhood home, I was thankful. Thankful my parents and family were close by. Thankful for enough progress for Adalee to move onto rehabilitation, and thankful for a husband and partner I could count on and who I deeply trusted. As I stood in the city's reflection, I spent time with the Lord processing my thoughts and realizing there was so much for which I was thankful. I could feel my spirit standing on Gods promises even though we were facing the unknown. I had listened to the feedback from the team of professionals that day. I was resolved to follow through on their instruction. My goal was to get Adalee to the point where she was comfortable walking in a brace or with a walker. I was determined to do everything I could to help her reach this goal. I would work hard to help her, but the truth was I had no control over the situation. The only thing I could do was focus on the blessings that surrounded us. I left the rest of the work in the hands of our healer. Only He could offer her the type of recovery that would give her a normal life. I was willing to accept how our life would be different, but then prayed the Lord would help Adalee recover her abilities.

Application

During a crisis we often face many unknowns, as well as deal with losses, fears, and grief. Tragedy is capable of lingering like a dark cloud and will overshadow the good things in our life. Finding ways to "rejoice in all circumstances" means taking the focus off our loss and casting light on the blessings we still have. Finding ways to rejoice also helps us to focus on eternal joy that Christ offers us through salvation. Finding ways to be thankful helps us shift our focus to the good things in our life and allows the hope of Jesus Christ to light our path moving forward. It is not God's will for us to be devastated. However, it is God's will for us to continually pray and seek Him in all circumstances. If we allow ourselves to practice finding ways to be thankful and rejoice in the Lord, it will draw us closer to him, and being in union with the Lord is His will for us.

Questions

1. List the blessings for which you are thankful.

2. How does finding ways to be thankful help you and your mindset?

3. Do you feel closer to the Lord when you rejoice in His goodness and give thanks?

Prayer

Lord, thank You for wanting to be close to me. Thank you for all the blessings in my life. I rejoice in You and thank You for everlasting hope. I pray Your hope will bring me peace and light the way for me to focus on how to give thanks in all circumstances. I pray for an attitude of contentment that rests on your sovereignty.

Nothing Is Impossible With God

Devotion 17

Luke 1:37

"For nothing is impossible with God."

New International Version

T he next morning was Saturday. I woke with pain and swelling in my throat. I knew I had come down with strep throat. Since I was a caregiver and not a patient in the rehabilitation center, I had to leave and get treated at a primary care facility. Adalee was scheduled to have her first *Physical Therapy* session that morning. The therapist would assess what needed to be done in order to set a plan in place to help Adalee walk. My hope was for Adalee to be stable enough to walk with a brace or a walker by the time she was released from the in-patient rehabilitation center. I had been given every indication from the experts this type of recovery would take time. This first therapy session was important, but I also had to get treated for my own sickness so I could stay with my daughter. I arranged for my parents to accompany Adalee to her physical therapy appointment while I went to the doctor. When I left my dad was carrying Adalee down the hallway to her session because she could not walk.

It took over two hours by the time I arrived at the clinic, received treatment, and made my way back to *"Our Children's House"*. I quickly made my way to the therapy rooms that were set up like a small gymnasium and clothed in bright red padded walls and floors. I walked through automated doors just as Adalee's first session ended. I found my parents standing and cheering while my dad played a video of Adalee running and walking on his cell phone. Adalee was standing next to my parents. Not only was she standing, she was walking! I was in a dumb founded state of shock. My heart was met with both relief and wonder. My parents explained what happened and replayed the video of how Adalee started running during her therapy session. The physical therapist was able to play with Adalee in a way that motivated her to get up and run. The session had ended, and the therapist was now gone. My dad told me the therapist who worked with Adalee oversaw *Physical Therapy* for the different centers for the entire healthcare network, which consisted of a very large hospital with multiple locations. On the weekends, different therapists under the *Baylor Health Care* system would conduct weekend shifts in place of the therapists who were present during the week. I did not retain the name or position of the man who worked with Adalee that Saturday morning. I asked about him several times, and no one on the staff seemed to know his name. We never saw him again, and I never had the opportunity to thank him. We walked down the corridor and made our way to Adalee's room. She walked the entire way while holding my dad's hand for stability. My two-year-old had not walked in three weeks, and during her first therapy session got up and started running. Was this normal? Is this the way children recover? Is this quick response typical? It did not seem usual based on the staff's reactions. Their responses indicated they were not used to seeing a child recover the ability to walk so quickly, but no one could define it. I was bewildered yet knew in my heart we watched God's answered prayer unfold before our eyes. I thanked the Lord from the depths of my soul. I did not need a definition or explanation because God made it apparent that "*nothing is impossible with God*". Humble gratitude overcame me. I had prayed in faith and asked for Adalee's full recovery, but I was bewildered. I recognized God granted healing that was undeniable. The fact Adalee was walking did not mean she would not need a lot of therapy to improve her stability and muscle tone. She was still not talking, and our work was just beginning. But the fact she was stable enough to get up, run, and begin walking on her own was an obvious manifestation of God's infinite ability.

Application

We do not always know how God will answer our prayers, but we can pray with faith and believe that *"Nothing is impossible with God."* God's incredible power can be displayed in any way. In the verse Jeremiah 32:27, God's word is revealed to the prophet Jeremiah and says *"I am the Lord, the God of all mankind. Is anything too hard for me?"* It is challenging to remember God's power is endless. In the *New Testament* and book of Matthew, Jesus tells his disciples in chapter 19 verse 26 *"..with God all things are possible."*. God's power is immeasurable. Many times, God's power is manifested in ways that brings instant improvement or immediate change. Other times, God's power is used in ways we may not always see as clearly. When we pray, we can have faith and know God is listening. Sometimes God may offer a solution or an escape to our problems or pain. Other times, God may offer help in times of trouble. Either way He hears us and acts on our behalf. God's divine nature is to work in our hearts and lives to build our faith, as well as the faith of others. We can praise God and cherish the times when we are blessed with the opportunity to see a supernatural display of his power.

Questions

1. What is your initial response when you hear a story of how God's power is displayed in a way for you to see and experience?

2. How would you apply the verse Luke 1:37 to your circumstances?

3. How do the verses Luke 1:37 and Matthew 19:26 challenge your faith?

Prayer

Lord, thank You for answering our prayers. Help me to pray with faith that truly believes "nothing is impossible" for You. Help me to see You working and displaying Your power in my life. Help me to pray boldly and to receive Your blessing with a humble heart.

Healing

Devotion 18

Philippians 3:21

"But our citizenship is in heaven. And we eagerly await a Savior from there, the Lord Jesus Christ, who, by the power that enables him to bring everything under his control, will transform our lowly bodies so that they will be like his glorious body."
New International Version

My cup spilled over with gratefulness as I continued to process the fact Adalee was walking. The staff was still concerned Adalee would fall because she had a slight limp, but she was hard to contain. She was still unable to speak and could not use her right arm, but she was determined to run. I felt the delicate balance of being thankful for the miraculous jump start given to my two-year-old yet remained focused on what was necessary to offer the best possible recovery for my daughter. My heart overflowed with awe, and I felt a profound thankfulness that reached an emotional depth I had never experienced. Praising God for what He has done in our life is important and scriptural. However, I was acutely aware that we were in a children's rehabilitation center with many children undergoing therapies for many reasons. Many of the children would have life-long challenges. I felt the weight of understanding the balance of openly giving thanks versus offering an intimate and personal prayer of gratitude. I felt a sacred and heavy responsibility to use the word "healing" in a respectful manner. I did not want to suppress the blessings we received, but I did want to honor the fact that God's plan for everyone is different. We were humbled our prayers were being answered in the way we hoped but understood there are times in life when things do not turn out the way we want. Mark and I had previously experienced situations where we did not receive the desired results or answer to our prayers. We both had lost loved ones to cancer and tragedy. During this time, Mark's mother, Rosemary, had battled brain cancer for eight years and was not getting well. The previous month she also suffered a stroke due to years of chemo and radiation. Even though we prayed her treatment would cure the cancer, her body was weakening, and she was now in a wheelchair. During this time of physical and emotional pain for his family, God's presence was real and tangible. Rosemary's, sickness did not weaken her faith. Her faith was steadfast as she leaned into the Lord to hold her up during a difficult disease. We witnessed how God was working in the lives of friends and family who prayed for her. The Lord used modern medicine to extend her life another decade so she could meet her grandchildren. Ultimately, her perfect healing was her transition from her earthly existence into the realm of eternity.

Application

The bible displays many stories of miracles, but the subject of healing can be difficult to understand. It is hard to comprehend why some can overcome sickness, and some do not. It can seem confusing and unfair for those that pray for healing and do not receive it in the way they hope. It can bring comfort to understand healing can be received in different ways. Healing can be received physically, spiritually, or emotionally. We traditionally think of healing as overcoming a physical sickness or disease, but healing can be a release from emotional bondage, freedom from addiction, or can take shape in the form of restoration by offering forgiveness or repairing a heart from a broken relationship. In the scripture Jesus used physical healing to represent the spiritual healing He offers through salvation. Jesus has the authority to heal our souls from sin and spiritual death. Our ultimate healing takes place when we leave this earthly realm and experience healing in its purest form in eternity with Jesus Christ. The process of healing can begin when we experience God while dealing with our pain. Even when our prayers are not answered the way we hope, we can receive incredible blessings when our focus is on Jesus Christ. Being open to what the Lord is teaching us through the journey draws us close to Him, which can result in spiritual or emotional healing. Experiencing God's presence alone is miraculous. If we believe Jesus is our Savior, we will inherit eternal life with Christ, and are offered eternal healing we cannot see through human flesh.

Questions

1. Have you witnessed or received healing? Is it physical, emotional, or spiritual?

2. Have you or someone you know prayed for healing? What was the outcome?

3. Has your faith been strengthened during this process?

Prayer

Lord, You are the God of miracles. Thank you for being the ultimate healer. You are the creator of the universe and have ultimate power. I pray for healing to take place in my life and in my heart. Help me eyes to see You working regardless of the physical outcome. May I experience Your presence in this journey, and I thank You that Your strength sustains me.

Glorifying God Through Difficulty

Devotion 19

1 Corinthians 10:31
"Whatever you do, do it for the glory of God"
New International Version

I n our normal life, our bedtime routine with our children included reading stories from age-appropriate children's books. We read the same books so often the kids would memorize them. We would use this time to teach them words and colors as the kids were learning how to talk. Adalee and I developed a game during our reading time where I would read a sentence and she would say the last word. It was a fun way to develop her speech as a toddler.

Adalee's physical progress in the first week of being admitted to the rehabilitation center was stunning, but her speech therapy sessions had not gone well, and she was still not talking. Her two-year-old nature was not cooperative in those initial speech sessions. One evening, as we settled into the rocking chair in Adalee's hospital room, I decided to play our reading game in hopes she might speak for me using words she previously memorized. I hoped it might trigger her brain and she would respond without thinking. It seemed like a long shot, but I thought I may as well try. My parents were present, as they were every evening. As I began to read Dr. Seuss's *"Hop on Pop"* Adalee began to speak by saying the last word of each sentence. The first time she spoke my mother gasped with excitement and my heart melted with relief. I held back tears and kept reading. Adalee was speaking familiar words and spoke the last words of each sentences. Our reading game worked and Adalee began to speak. Some of her words were slurred, but we watched how her brain and will worked together. It was like turning on a switch. We listened and watched as she made progress. My parents continued to come to the hospital each evening after my mom got off work. A couple nights later I was getting Adalee ready for bed and I laid her down to change her diaper. In her two-year-old voice she began to sing. Her words sounded like a sweet little hum, but the melody was recognizable. Adalee was singing a song from a children's praise CD we listened to frequently. She was able to sing the words she had previously memorized. The title of the song was *"Be Glorified"*. The words to the song are *"In my life Lord, be glorified, be glorified. In my life Lord, be glorified in me"*. My parents and I looked at one another in amazement as this sweet praise song flowed from her voice and heart. Once again, my parents and I were deeply moved. I was reminded by my toddler to give God glory, and to let the Lord be glorified through this situation. My mother said, *"this is the perfect song for her life."* It was a precious notification that her testimony would give God glory in that moment and in her life for years to come.

Be Glorified
by Ernie Rettino & Debie Kerner

In my life Lord be glorified, be glorified
In my life Lord be glorified in me.
In my heart Lord, be glorified, be glorified
In my heart Lord, be glorified in me.
In my home Lord, be glorified, be glorified
In my home Lord, be glorified in me.
In my church Lord, be glorified, be glorified
In my church Lord, be glorified in me.
In my school Lord, be glorified, be glorified
In my school Lord, be glorified in me.

Application

God wants to show us His glory because He is good, and He loves us. God desires us to experience the sweet, tenderness of his Holy Spirit. God can take any circumstance and transform it into a beautiful depiction of his grace, love, power, and forgiveness. When we apply the verse 1 Corinthians 10:31 to our lives we are opening ourselves up for the Lord to work and be glorified through us. Abiding by this verse also helps guide us as we make choices. When we pour God's truth into our mind it will spill over from our heart into our reactions in any given situation. When we are intertwined with the Holy Spirit our communion with the Lord can take place anytime and anywhere. We cannot control everything that happens in life, but we can choose how we respond. We can ask ourselves the question, *"Do our actions, speech, or choices glorify God?".*

Questions

1. How does this verse impact your perspective on how to make choices?

2. How does this verse impact your perspective on how you respond to your difficult circumstances?

3. How do you think the Lord can use your situation to bring Him glory?

Prayer

Lord, I submit myself and my circumstances to You. I pray You will be glorified in my life. I ask You will be glorified even as I am hurting and walking through this hard journey. Help me to make choices that point me to You.

Dicsipline

Devotion 20

Hebrews 12:2

"Let us fix our eyes on Jesus, the author and perfecter of our faith, who for the joy set before him endured the cross, scorning its shame, and sat down at the right hand of the throne of God".

New International Version

The year of 2011 was busy and filled with major life transitions. We moved across country, had a third child, managed a career change, and made additions to my business while transitioning a three and four-year-old to a new home and school. The changes were an outcome of prayer, allowed us to move closer to family, and included a sweet new baby girl for which we knew was God's plan. Even though each transition was a blessing, it was a lot to handle in a short period of time and I was making my way through the newborn fog of little sleep. Meeting the needs of a new baby caused mornings to be quite difficult. I struggled to get the kids to preschool on time and was trying to manage all the changes related to my business and new home. Exhaustion began to blur my view of the blessings God had given us. In a desperate effort to salvage my attitude I began to recite Psalm 118:24 out loud in the car each morning when I took the kids to preschool. *"This is the day the Lord has made.* (no matter what) *Let us rejoice and be glad in it".* Many mornings, I forced myself to say the verse because I knew I needed it. I was tired and overwhelmed, but as the year progressed, my effort to cope and maintain a positive attitude turned into a discipline. Quoting this verse in the car each morning transformed my perspective and evolved into an opportunity to teach my young children scripture. I became accustomed to rejoicing in the Lord for who He is regardless of my feelings or circumstance. I began to sense the Lord was preparing me for something. Little did I know what was in store. Psalm 118:24 came to my mind when I was in the *Pediatric Intensive Unit* with Adalee. I realized how God had disciplined me for the past two years, and it helped me understand how He was using the discipline to sustain me. This verse helped me to remember to thank God for being who He is even as my child was dealing with a life-threatening situation.

Application

Discipline is not easy or comfortable, but we can allow it to help us grow. God uses discipline to grow us spiritually. Ephesians 12:2 says God is the *"author and perfecter of our faith"*. God uses spiritual disciplines to build and strengthen our faith. Gods purpose for discipline is sanctification which is the process by which a believer conforms more to the image of Christ. Spiritual discipline equips us with the knowledge and ability to apply what we learn in our everyday life, as well as in a difficult situation. The scripture tells us God loves us. The bible does not say the Lord brings turmoil upon our lives, but He will walk with us through hardships and use them to refine us. Hebrews 12:5-6 says *"...My son, do not make light of the Lord's discipline, and do not lose heart when he rebukes you, the Lord disciplines those he loves"*. The purpose of this verse is to communicate God loves for us, which is a fundamental reason He uses discipline in our lives. The purpose of discipline is to remove sin, protect us, challenge us to godliness, and to build our faith. In addition, Hebrews 12:7 says, *"Endure hardship as discipline, God is treating you as sons. For what son is not disciplined by his father?"*. Just like a loving parent who disciplines and guides a child, the Lord graciously deals with us. Our difficult circumstances are not God's punishment or wrath, but He uses those difficulties to fashion us into His likeness. Reading and digesting scripture daily will discipline our minds and hearts on how to view God and our circumstances.

Questions

1. How does the concept of discipline apply to what you are going through?

2. How has the scripture impacted how you are responding to God and your circumstances?

3. How have you been challenged?

4. Have you seen how discipline has improved your life and relationship with Jesus Christ?

Prayer

Lord, help me to walk in the discipline of reading Your word every day and applying it to my circumstances. Help me to remember every day is a gift from You, and to rejoice in Your goodness. Help me to see the areas where I struggle and help me to understand the lessons You are asking me to learn.

Obedience

Devotion 21

John 14:23
"Anyone who loves me will obey my teaching. My Father will love them, and we will come to them and make our home with them."

New International Version

During our time in the rehabilitation center, I continued to publish posts on our *Caring Bridge* blog to update family and friends on Adalee's progress. The Holy Spirit began to impress on me to share my testimony of Psalm 118:24. Initially, I did not feel comfortable sharing this story. I had already been open about how the Lord was ministering to us during this time. I did not want to over share, and I have never been a person to wear my emotions on my sleeve. Inviting others into an even deeper and more intimate spiritual lesson I was learning caused me to fear criticism that could easily be deflected right back into my soft spot. I was already tender, and my greatest concern was that I would be perceived as making the post about myself instead of my daughter. I chose not to share. I wanted to make sure I did not confuse my emotions with the Lord's prompting for fear my intentions would be received or taken in vain. For several days my soul continued to feel hard-pressed. I felt as though someone was kneading dough in my stomach. The Holy Spirit was pressing in, and I could not shake it. One evening, after a week of feeling this pressure grow, I laid in the darkness of the hospital room and prayed, *"Lord, sharing this testimony is vulnerable and scary. I need a sign. If You want me to share it on this public blog, please show me and make it very clear."*

Every morning during our stay at *"Our Children's House"*, Adalee received a breakfast tray. On the tray was a scripture and prayer written on a tiny card. The next morning, after I prayed for a sign, Adalee's breakfast tray was delivered. The scripture on the tray was Psalm 118:24 *"This is the day the Lord had made, let us rejoice and be glad in it."* The Lord gave me an answer and literally served me a confirmation on a "silver platter". God's tangible response left no doubt I was supposed to share my testimony. The prayer that was written on the card that day said, *"God of all faithfulness, break the shackles of my past and dispel any dread of the future; then I will be empowered to live well this day."* Amen.

I did not know the reason I was supposed to share, but the Lord empowered me to understand that "knowing" was not my job. I was learning that God had a purpose, and my responsibility was to simply obey. God was calling me to share publicly, and I needed to trust Him. As I wrote the blog, I began to face the fact I may never know how God would use my testimony. This process of obedience was hard and nerve wracking, but as I followed through and typed the words, I felt a peace.I was learning to trust the Lord and be o.k. with the idea I may never know how it might impact someone. It could be for one person or many, and I had to be o.k. with not knowing. As I published the post, I released it into the Lords hands, and would not have to think or worry about it again. It was a lesson of trust and obedience.

Application

Obedience is one of our expressions of love to the Lord. We have the choice to be followers of Christ and align our lives with scripture.The teachings of Jesus are outlined in the pages of God's word and act as a guide. John 14:23

clearly states that if we love Jesus, we will obey his teachings. Obedience can also necessitate diligent prayer to seek the counsel of the Holy Spirit as we make decisions for our lives. Acting in obedience is not always easy. Sometimes it calls us to step far out of our comfort zone and wade into uncharted waters. Many times, it requires us to be vulnerable and forces us to place complete faith in intangible ideas. It necessitates us to lean in on faith. Luke 11:28 says, *"Blessed rather are those who hear the Word of God and obey it."* Jesus spoke these words as he was addressing a group of people.In verse 27 a woman called out, *"Blessed is the woman who gave you birth and nursed you"*. The woman was offering a compliment or blessing to Jesus. He was speaking to a group of people in a culture who placed the highest value on family. They believed their lineage guaranteed they were a part of God's chosen people, the Israelites. Although family is very important, Jesus's response told them that a person's obedience to God should be our highest priority, which was communicating that following Christ was a personal decision.

There are incredible blessings when we strive to be obedient followers of Christ. No one is perfect, but the Lord can identify a heart willing to serve Him.

Questions

1. What is your response to Luke 11:28?

2. How does obedience apply when you are dealing with a crisis?

3. Have you felt the Lord call you to be obedient in a way that has caused you discomfort?

Prayer

God of all faithfulness, break the shackles of my past and dispel any dread of the future; then I will be empowered to live well this day." Amen.

Give Grace

2 Corinthians 12:9

"...My grace is sufficient for you, for my power is made perfect in weakness."
New International Version

After only four weeks of inpatient therapy Adalee was released from the children's rehabilitation hospital. Our hearts were grateful. Adalee had overcome all odds and was walking, talking, running, and beginning to use her right arm and hand. We drove home to Waco and felt relief to be with Mark, Seth, and Hannah Grace. We were greeted by a loving church, community, and friends who brought a few meals for the week. Mark and the kids had not missed a beat. Mark had the entire house cleaned when we arrived. Seth and Hannah Grace did well at school thanks to their teachers who were so nurturing. Their sweet teachers cared for them in a way that put me at ease. I will forever have an incredible sense of thankfulness and love toward each care giver who kept them emotionally confident enough to continue to learn and develop at school while I was away. Adalee and I adjusted to being back home and all five of us settled into our new routine. We hit the ground running. Adalee began her follow-up visits and outpatient assessments and therapies three days per week. The routine of getting my work done and taking care of my family was intensified by adding multiple days of therapy and doctor's appointments to our schedule. Our days were packed full and there was only room for a very structured schedule to make sure I was getting everything done. I began to wake up at 5:00 a.m. to get my work out in. I knew this was a way to care for myself and keep my mind and body healthy after being under so much stress. Even though the transition was smooth it was hard to assess a situation we had never been in and articulate if everyone was doing well. Emotions eventually surfaced into some difficult moments where I realized the kids were adjusting to having me home. They had done great under the circumstances but painting a perfect picture would do us all a dis-service. One evening tension between me and one of the kids mounted. Mark looked at me and said, *"they are adjusting to you being home".* I had to remember that on the outside they appeared to be unaltered, but that did not mean they had not experienced emotions or fear during the two months where I was gone. It was apparent we all needed a lot more grace than usual.

Application

During times of crisis everyone is affected. We cope in our own ways and need the grace of God and others around us to give us the space to deal with our emotions. Even when things seem to take a turn for the better, we must take time to let ourselves and our loved ones process the events that have taken place. There will be times of adjustment, and everyone processes things differently. There will also be times when we think we are fine, and then we will surprise ourselves when we or a loved one acts out or has a meltdown. When all else fails offer grace. God's grace is enough in all moments and on all occasions. Jesus saved us and offered the ultimate grace we do not deserve by dying on the cross for our sins. We can receive the grace Jesus has given us, and then in turn give it others. In 2 Corinthians 12:9 Jesus also stated that His *"power is made perfect in our weakness".* We can give moments where grace is needed to the Lord and allow Him to fashion something strong and beautiful from our pain and weakness.

Questions

1. Have you been able to give yourself grace during your crisis?

2. Have you been able to extend grace to others?

3. How has the Lord made His *"power perfect in your weakness"*?
   What does mean to you?

Prayer

Lord, thank You for giving me Your saving grace. Please help me to recognize when others need grace and help me to give it freely. Help me to also accept when I need to give myself grace. I pray Your power will be made perfect in my weakness.

God Is Always Working

Devotion 23

Philippians 1:6
"Being confident of this, that he who began a good work in you will carry it on to completion until the day of Christ Jesus."

New International Version

Four months earlier in the month of December, I was having breakfast with three of my girlfriends. As we huddled in a booth at a favorite local eatery, my friend Shelley announced she was pregnant with her fourth child. We celebrated her exciting news Texas style with breakfast tacos.

The weeks after Adalee and I returned home were filled with spring festivities celebrating the end of the school year for Seth and Hannah Grace. I took time one morning to help Seth's first grade teacher at *Field Day*. During the middle of the activities, God gave me a full view into how he had been working. On the school field where the elementary aged kids were racing, competing, and enjoying games I saw my friend Shelley. Since I had been away, Shelley had blossomed into her third trimester. With excitement and anticipation, I asked *"Do you know what you are having?"* Without hesitation she said, *"it is a girl, but she is not going to live."* My heart sank and the excited shrills of children faded into the distance. For the next few moments, I stood in shock trying to find the right words as Shelley explained the baby's condition. The baby's lungs were not developing properly and would not sustain her once she was born. I had just experienced a life-threatening situation with my child, but I was speechless and felt ill-equipped to offer an appropriate response. I could not find the right words for my friend who was about to lose her baby. Standing next to the playground, Shelley told me she had been struggling until she read my *Caring Bridge* post on Psalm 118:24. Her next words astounded me. Shelley looked directly into my eyes and said, *"I read your post that day, and it changed my whole perspective."* Tears welled up in my soul even though my face did not show them. I realized the post I felt compelled to share a month earlier was specifically for my friend. Shelley was about to lose her baby and was walking in faith to let the Lord sustain her. In return, the Lord used Shelley to minister to me. The Lord allowed me to see why He wanted me to share my testimony on Psalm 118:24. Maybe it was for Shelley alone, or maybe it was for more than one person. I may never know but seeing the fruit of how the Lord was working in this situation deepened my trust and ability to listen and respond to the Holy Spirit. It taught me when I feel God's prompting my job is to simply obey and let Him do the rest.

Application

In Philippians 1:6 the apostle Paul is describing the process of growth and maturity that takes place as a Christian. The process begins when we believe in Jesus and continues through our lifetime until meet him face to face. The purpose is for us to know Jesus Christ and to become more like Him. We are a work in progress and the Lord will use personal situations to sharpen and refine us. The Lord is always at work and ministers in ways we cannot fathom and often in ways we cannot see. We also never know when the Lord will use our own pain to bring comfort or encouragement to someone else. We can pray and ask the Lord to use our crisis to help others. Even if someone's difficulty seems harder than our own, the Lord can still use us to minister and support one another. When we feel ill-equipped or unworthy of a task, we must not let our feelings of inadequacy hold us back from following through on what the Lord asks us to do. The power of the Holy Spirit intercedes and works in unimaginable ways. God is always working on our behalf whether it is to build our faith, or the faith of someone else.

Questions

1. What is your response to Philippians 1:6?

2. Do you immediately apply this verse to your current crisis or to someone you know?

3. Have you ever held back on reaching out to someone because you felt inadequate?

4. How do you feel about asking the Holy Spirit to give you strength to step out of your comfort zone?

Prayer

Lord, thank You for the confidence You give us through your word. Thank You for helping me grow into the Christ follower You have called me to be. May I see how the power of the Holy Spirit is at work and building the kingdom of heaven in my life and those around me.

God Cares for the Brokenhearted

Featuring Shelley Reeves
Devotion 24

Psalm 34:18
"The Lord is close to the brokenhearted and saves those who are crushed in spirit."
New International Version

During the fall of 2013, my husband Matt and I discussed whether we were going to try to have a fourth child. Because of my age we had concerns. We already had three beautiful, healthy girls, Kelsey, McKenzie, and Ainsley. *"Were we being greedy to ask for another baby?"* I was getting older and faced the reality of potential health risks for myself and a baby. Together we prayed and decided we would try to have a baby for three months. Our true desire was to make the right decision, so we also prayed for a confirmation. We prayed that if having a fourth baby was God's will, He would allow us to know by the end of the year. The very next month I became pregnant and Baby Reeves number four was due at the end of August 2014. We were thrilled and so thankful. The first half of my pregnancy was completely normal. Then, on March 8th, 2014, I had my twenty-week checkup. The ultrasound technician was very quiet throughout the exam and said very little. After he finished the ultrasound, he asked me to wait for the doctor in his office. By this point, my heart was racing, and I began to imagine the worst. However, nothing could have prepared me for the news we received. The doctor explained I had almost no amniotic fluid which was preventing the development of the baby's lungs. Without amniotic fluid and underdeveloped lungs, the baby would not survive. The doctor gave me the number of a specialist and told me to make an appointment for the next day. The next day the specialist explained the baby's kidneys were not working properly causing me to have no amniotic fluid. Without amniotic fluid, the baby's lungs could not form properly. He went on to explain that if we did not terminate the pregnancy, the pregnancy could continue to term, and the baby would die soon after birth because it would not be able to breath on its own. The doctor explained it was our choice. In our minds, terminating the pregnancy was not an option. We would pray for a miracle until God told us otherwise. We left the ultrasound room, and I went to get blood work done. We wanted to know the sex of the baby so we could pray for him or her by name. It took ten days to receive the blood results. I prayed daily that it would be a girl. I knew how much my husband Matt wanted a son, and I did not want him to lose the son his heart desired. The next few days were a blur. We endured the heartache of telling our girls the baby they were so excited about was going to die. Word spread among friends and our church. Our community was praying on our behalf, but no one could understand what we were experiencing. I was home alone when I got the call from the hospital to let me know the results of the blood work. I remember the nurse on the phone saying *"Mrs. Reeves, congratulations it's a girl."* I cried and cried and thanked God for answering my prayer. We immediately named her Caroline.

Application

God always hears our prayers and knows the intimate details of what we are going through. The Lord will *"draw near to us"* and respond in ways we understand so we can recognize His presence. We may wish and pray to be rescued from pain and may pray to escape the unbearable. Even if our sadness is not taken away God promises to be the source of strength, comfort, and courage. He will walk us through our sickness, loss, or grief. When we seek the Lord, He will give our weary souls strength and will fill our broken hearts with His unwavering love. You may feel crushed by the weight of sorrow, but the living God saves us through His compassion, grace, and sacrifice.

Questions

1. How has the Lord drawn near to you if your prayers have not been answered in the way you hoped?

2. How has your heart, life, or spirit been lifted or encouraged by scripture?

3. Has the Lord shown you a situation where Psalm 34:18 seems tangible?

Prayer

Lord, thank You for ministering to my broken heart and lifting my spirit when my soul is crushed by pain and circumstance. I pray I will feel Your presence lift me up during this time of grief and sadness. My I put my hope in Jesus Christ, and I hold onto Your truth. Fill my heart with Your love so that I may receive Your grace.

God Is Good All of The Time

Featuring Shelley Reeves
Devotions 25

Psalm 118:24
"This is the day the Lord has made; I will rejoice and be glad in it."
New International Version

Not long before we found out the news about Caroline, Adalee suffered a stroke. I followed Sarah's *Caring Bridge* blog daily to get updates on Adalee. During the weeks after Caroline's diagnosis, I read Sarah's post and testimony about Psalm 118:24. In her entry, she described how she and her kids recited this verse in the car every day. Reading her testimony gave me a completely new perspective and attitude regarding my pregnancy. Through her story and scripture, the Lord had encouraged me and given me something to hold on to. From that point forward I felt a peace. I was confused and sad, but I was going to rejoice with each new day. The spring flew by, and the pregnancy seemed normal, except it was not. I reached the mark of being thirty-four weeks pregnant. Every month we heard the baby's heartbeat during our doctor appointments and could see she was growing. I desperately wanted Caroline to be born alive, but with each week that passed there was a greater chance she would pass away. My oldest daughter, Kelsey, was scheduled to go to summer camp with friends the week of June 22nd. I went to my doctor appointment the week before and decided to let Kelsey go to camp and planned to induce when she returned. On the morning of June 25th, I woke up and knew something was different. I called Matt at work and told him to come home immediately. This could not be happening. Kelsey was at camp three hours away, and my daughter McKenzie was at my parents. I was on day three of potty-training my two-year-old daughter. I thought *"Surely God would not let this happen today. This was not what we had planned. Today was not the right day".* We rushed to the hospital and were able to stop labor until our friends and family could arrive. In the middle of a massive, Texas sized thunderstorm, Caroline Elizabeth Reeves was born. Caroline came into this world crying. She was alive, which was a huge answer to prayer. She weighed three pounds, seven ounces and had a head full of curly hair. Caroline looked just like her sisters. We spent the next several hours loving on her and thanking God for the few hours of her life. The girls were able to give her a bath and we took the opportunity to take family pictures. There were no rules. We could keep Caroline with us for as long as we needed. After spending these precious moments together with family and friends, our loved ones began to leave. Together in the stillness, Matt and I treasured our time with our baby. We took many pictures and recorded her hand and footprints. I then made the hardest phone call I have ever made in my life. I called the nurse to let her know we were ready to let her go. We dressed her, wrapped her in a blanket, gave her kisses, and then handed her to the nurse. The nurse gently took Caroline into her arms, turned around, and walked out of the room. In a matter of twelve hours, we had arrived at the hospital, given birth, said goodbye to our daughter, and walked out a back entrance with empty arms.

After spending a few hours at my parent's house with family and friends, we made our way back to our home. I felt numb and was in a state of shock. The day did not seem real. *"How could it be over?". "My baby was safe inside me.", "Why did it have to end?"* were the thoughts racing through my mind. I remember climbing into bed having no idea how to move forward. I did the only thing I could think to do and grabbed my daily devotional from my nightstand. When I turned to June 25th, the verse for the day was Psalm 118:24. *"This is the day the Lord has made; I will rejoice and be glad in it".* Chills. Tears. This day that initially felt so wrong was perfectly picked by God. The verse Sarah shared in her blog post that completely changed my perspective was the verse of the day on June 25th, Caroline's birthday, and homecoming. I knew this was not a coincidence. I still have the text message I sent Sarah at 11:31 p.m. on June 25th saying, *"you will never believe this! How can anyone doubt how great God is?"* We watched how God worked in our lives and revealed himself to us through the scripture on that sacred day.

On June 9th, 2016, 16 days before Caroline's 2nd birthday, we welcomed our son Austin Blake Reeves to our family. For me, Austin represents hope, trust, faith, and healing. He is a true gift from God to say I love you and I work everything for good. God is good all the time, even when we do not understand.

Application

Praising God and rejoicing in his goodness may feel like the last thing we want to do when we are grief stricken or consumed with sorrow. However, we can be honest before the Lord, and as we express our heart God can take our prayers of need and help us find a reason to rejoice. When we make the choice to *"rejoice in the Lord"* for who He is our eyes are opened to a new perspective. God's goodness may be the only thing that is constant in our lives on any given day. This world is always changing. Remembering to praise God reminds us of His unchanging love and gives us hope. Regardless of what happens to us God is always good. He finds ways to reveal His goodness to reach us, and to offer His tender spirit to minister to us. Every day is a *"day the Lord has made"*, and that alone is a reminder of His greatness. God is always worthy of our praise even on the hardest days.

Questions

1. Have you had a day where the last thing you want to do is rejoice like Psalm 118:24 says to do?

2. Has the Lord used the combination of circumstances and a verse to minister to you in your grief?

3. Are you allowing yourself to accept grief and work through it?

Prayer

Lord, I thank You I can rejoice in your goodness. Thank You that today is a gift from You. Help me to see Your goodness shine a light into my sorrow. I pray that as I rejoice in Your goodness You will help me to have a fresh perspective and to see the joy only You can bring during this difficult time.

God's Perfect Timing

Devotion 26

Ecclesiastes 3: 1-8

"There is a time for everything and a season for every activity under the heavens; a time to be born and a time to die, a time to plant and a time to uproot,a time to kill and a time to heal, a time to tear down and a time build, a time to weep and a time to laugh, a time to mourn and a time to dance,a time to scatter stones and time to gather them, a time to embrace and a time to refrain from embracing, a time to search and a time to give up, and time to keep and a time to throw away, a time to tear down and a time to mend, a time to be silent and a time to speak, a time to love and a time to hate, a time for war and a time for peace."

New International Version

L ife moves forward, and we must move with it. As we transitioned into our new normal Adalee was doing well. However, there were still issues to face, physical hurtles for Adalee to overcome, and countless hours of therapy for the next two and half years. There was time for reflection and learning lessons from a process that would not end just because Adalee was able to be home. From the outside looking in it seemed as though we were back to a normal routine. The time and financial commitment it took to make sure our child received ongoing intervention was not necessarily easy to see from the outside in. Adalee was able to do most things a child her age could do but there were still limitations. As parents our goal was to help her develop as any other child her own age. We intentionally lived life and maintained certain activities for the family. At the same time, we had to be watchful and considered each activity and the potential risk of another head injury. It required a vigilant recall of every rule and piece of advice the doctor's presented, while maintaining a positive outlook and communicating to Adalee she could do anything if she set her mind to it. For the next couple of years, it was as if we put our heads down and barreled headfirst into our goals and demanding schedule. We progressed, but our daughter was still in the process of recovery and our emotions were still very raw. At every step, I would mentally process what we all had gone through but had to focus on doing whatever we needed to do for our daughter to develop to the best of her ability. It took over a year for me to get to a point where I could let down, and then I began to process all that had taken place. There were still many things to learn, and ways to watch God work. I had no idea how deep God would take us. I learned to walk through stages of grief. Initially, I thought experiencing grief came after the loss of a loved one. It was a crazy notion for me as I had not lost my child. Here we were as a family living a "normal life" for which we are very thankful. Emotionally, we were able to press on, but there were days where I had to give my emotions some grace. I experienced moments where I felt sad. I then felt guilty for feeling sad when my child had received healing and recovered far beyond what the doctors predicted. I learned it was normal to feel those emotions and remember the situation was very serious. I also realized I was dealing with emotions I did not have time to manage in the hospital. I learned to recognize the emotional, physical, and mental commitment it took for our family to make some life adjustments to give Adalee the resources she needed. I learned to allow myself to face those emotions while making the choice not to allow bitterness or sadness to overshadow the abundant blessings. As the primary caregiver, it was imperative I recognize the toll a situation like this takes to make sure I was getting the rest I needed mentally and physically.

Application

There is a season for everything. Ecclesiastes 3:1-8 lays out the cycles of life. Each stage affords us the space and time to work, sow, reap rewards, rejoice, deal with inevitable problems, and to process what we have been through mentally and emotionally. Allowing ourselves time to grieve and mourn is healthy and biblical, but we also must move forward to heal, dance, and laugh. We cannot stay in the same place forever. God wants us to embrace the next stage with faith and trust that no matter what happens He provides us with what we need. When we put our faith in Jesus Christ, we can trust God's timing is perfect and know difficult times can refine us to come out on the other side having learned to see God's blessings. God will take our sorrow and in due time help us experience joy. The words in Ecclesiastes give us the grace to move through different emotions. Denying ourselves time to properly mourn a loss, grieve a relationship, or adjust to a new situation is not healthy. When we suppress pain, we do not face it, which will prevent us from learning and growing. The difficult cycles of life should not prevent us from believing in God. We can view hardship as a way to discover how to trust in God and find joy in the process of growth. We must offer ourselves space to search, refrain, and to be still. We must give our heart and mind a chance to reset and mend in order to be able to embrace how to grow spiritually from dealing with the difficult cycles of life. Time has a way of happening. When we are in the middle of a perfect storm our view is usually clouded by the pain of circumstance. We may not fully understand how God's perfect timing applies to our situation until we can look back and see His hand with the clear vision hindsight offers.

Questions

1. How do you apply the cycles of life in *Ecclesiastes* to your own circumstances?

2. Have you given yourself grace to acknowledge which stage of grief you are experiencing?

3. How do you think God' perfect timing will help you in your own situation?

Prayer

Lord, thank You for giving us time. Help me to identify how I need to use my time wisely to heal, adjust, and move forward. I pray for discernment to know how to be healthy spiritually, emotionally, and physically.

Run The Race

Devotion 27

2 Timothy 4:7-8
"I have fought the fight, I have finished the race, I have kept the faith. Now there is in store for me the crown of righteousness, which the Lord, the righteous judge, will award to me on that day – and not only to me, but also to all who have longed for his appearing."

New International Version

Monday, July 18th, 2016, was Adalee's last day of out patient therapy. Adalee was excited and we were all ready to begin a new chapter. For almost three years our weekly routine had been scheduled around Adalee's therapy. We thanked the Lord Adalee exceeded every goal set by her team of doctors. We were thankful for a great team of therapists, as well as for Adalee's determination to keep up with her older siblings, which also contributed to her improvement. Her final day of therapy encompassed a mixture of emotions intertwined with relief and gratitude. My heart began to let down and feel utterly grateful. Adalee would still have physical challenges to work on and will always have a slightly weaker right side which she pragmatically refers to as "righty", but she would go to school and have the same abilities as the other children. During these years, the Lord opened my eyes to how the tiniest details of this physical world represents the spiritual realm. Adalee's weaker side is a beautiful reminder that we all have faults. Adalee's "righty" symbolizes how we can offer grace to our physical imperfections. As a young child, Adalee's perspective was shaped to overcome her difficulties, which has fashioned her character and identity. We pray the Lord will continue to use those characteristics to fulfill the purpose and plan He has for her life.

Application

Storms come and go, and even when the crisis leaves a mark life goes on. The sun will rise, and the sun will set again. We have the choice to decide how we will continue living, and if we will forge ahead to live our life in the fullness of Jesus Christ. The book of 2 Timothy is written by the apostle Paul. He writes a farewell letter from a Roman prison on death row. Paul knew he was living his final days. His letter included encouragement to those who followed his ministry. He knew they had much life to live and offered advice and inspiration. Paul had followed Christ and his words in chapter 4 verses 7 & 8 outline a goal for how to live for Christ. He was able to look back on his life and know that even in his weakness he fought the good fight. He proclaimed his faith and confidence of knowing he would inherit a crown of righteousness given to us all through the sacrifice and resurrection of our Lord Jesus. Before Paul knew Jesus was the son of God, he persecuted Christians to the death. The Lord turned his life around and turned Paul's sins and weakness into one of the most inspiring representations of how to live a Christian life. Regardless of whether we have days or a lifetime to live, we can pursue a life in Christ Jesus where one day we can look back and proclaim with confidence that we have *"fought the fight, finished the race, and kept the faith."* We can let our circumstances and problems take over and negatively define us, or we can trust the Lord, give him our broken pieces, and let Him create a beautiful masterpiece. God will use our adversity to do a good work in us and fulfill His glorious plan for our life. God loves us and His purpose for our lives is to be in relationship with Him and to bring Him glory. Remembering that we have eternity with Christ gives us the strength to press on and overcome present struggles. Jesus has already won the victory.

He gives us strength to have faith and push forward. Press on. You have a race to run. You have a mark to make.

Questions

1. How have you grown during this time in your life?

2. How do you apply 2 Timothy 4:7-8 to your present and future?

3. What is God calling you to do?

4. How are you going to press on?

Prayer

Lord, thank You for giving us a hope and a future. Help me boldly live a life that is glorifying to You. Help me to accept the call You have placed on my life and to run the race you have set before me.

Praise The Lord

Devotion 28

Psalms 34: 1-3

"I will extol the name of the Lord at all time; His praise will always be on my lips. My soul will boast in the Lord; Let the afflicted hear and rejoice.Glorify the Lord with me; let us exalt His name together. I sought the Lord and He answered me, he delivered me from all my fears. Those who look to Him are radiant. Their faces are never covered with shame. This poor man called, and the Lord heard him; he saved him out of all his troubles. The angel of the Lord encamps around those who fear him, and he delivers them."

New International Version

From the moment the Lord whispered His word into our perfect storm I knew it was my joy and responsibility to praise Him and share of how He moved in our lives. We are grateful for all the Lord has done in our daughter's life, and for our family. I often read Psalm 34 to remind me to praise and thank God. We have so many blessings for which we are thankful. However, in our current world where things are chaotic and in constant motion it is easy for our human flesh to be distracted and lose focus on the blessings God has given.

This past year has been unprecedented for us all. Our entire world has been turned upside down as we have dealt with a pandemic. Many have lost loved ones, jobs, and have suffered greatly. We have all truly been through *A Perfect Storm*. Even through this time of uncertainty we can remember who God is and what He has done for us. We can look beyond our physical existence and remember we already have the victory in Jesus Christ.

Application

God is always good. He will always be there for us, show His goodness, deliver us, work in our hearts, and meet our needs. It is up to us to respond. To receive God's blessings takes our active participation and obedience to accept His goodness in our lives. Offering praise sets our minds on the goodness of God, renews our hope, and brings us joy. We can always start to see a light at the end of the tunnel when we open our hearts and emulate Psalm 34.

I pray this time has encouraged you. If you have experienced *A Perfect Storm*, I hope you have found strength in Jesus Christ. Every crisis and outcome are different, but we can all find refuge in the same place. Take time today to give thanks for all that the Lord has done in your life. Give Him glory for who He is, what He has done, and what He will continue to do.

To God be the Glory.

Questions

1. How can you praise God today?

2. How will you live your life differently as you move beyond your *Perfect Storm*?

3. How does Psalm 34 apply to your future?

Prayer

Lord, I praise You for being a God of love and mercy. Thank You for saving me from my difficulty and helping me to know how to better deal with life's circumstances. Thank You for your divine and loving nature. May my life reflect your glory, and may I praise You in words and actions.

Featured Guest

Shelley Reeves grew up in Waco, Texas where she lives with her husband Matt and their family.Shelley is the mother five children Kelsey, McKenzie, Ainsley, Caroline, and Austin.

After graduated from *Baylor University* with a degree in *Information Systems* Shelley moved to Dallas where she met her husband Matt. Matt and Shelley met at *Prestonwood Baptist Church* while playing in a softball league.

Shelley and Matt returned to Waco in 2012 to raise their family. Shelley works in the *Energy and Sustainability Services Division* for *Schneider Electric*.

Shelley and Matt stay very busy attending their kids sporting events and activities. The Reeves family loves to snow ski and enjoys the adventure of traveling.

About the Author

Sarah Nelson lives in Waco, Texas with her husband, Mark, and their three children Seth, Hannah Grace, and Adalee. Sarah is a *Contributing Writer* and *Influencer* for the online parenting publication *Waco Moms Blog* and was published in the *Roaring Lambs Ministry "Stories of Faith Volume II"* in 2017. Sarah has had the opportunity to speak to women's groups and events, and interviews on podcasts, radio, and televised segments to share her testimony and raise awareness to educate about the signs of strokes in children.

Sarah has a heart for music and has been gifted with opportunities to lead worship in different capacities since the age of thirteen. She has combined her passion and skill for writing to partner with organizations such as the *American Family Radio* and *Gospel Music Association*, while releasing original music as an independent artist within the *Christian Contemporary* genre.

Sarah graduated from *Baylor University* with a *BBA* in *Marketing*, has a background in business, and served at *First Woodway Baptist Church* as the *Connection Coordinator*.

Sarah loves to travel, water ski, snow ski, and adventuring with her family.

Made in the USA
Las Vegas, NV
28 February 2022

44737836R00062